ENGELMANN · Letters from
WITTGENSTEIN

PAUL ENGELMANN

Letters from

LUDWIG WITTGENSTEIN

With a Memoir

HORIZON PRESS

NEW YORK

© *Basil Blackwell, Oxford, 1967*
Library of Congress Catalog Card No. 68-14711
First published in 1968
in the United States by Horizon Press,
156 Fifth Avenue, New York, N.Y. 10010

Translated by L. FURTMÜLLER
Edited by B. F. McGUINNESS

PRINTED IN GREAT BRITAIN

To my Mother

Contents

Preface

Paul Engelmann was born at Olmütz (now Olomouc, Czechoslovakia) in June 1891. In this book he writes about his native town and its intellectual circle.

Paul Engelmann died in February 1965 at Tel Aviv, Israel, where since 1934 he had worked as an interior architect, written books and essays, and taken part in many philosophical and literary discussions. The present book, written during the last months of his life, has remained incomplete, as he was unable to add the intended account of some further meetings with Ludwig Wittgenstein, especially during the period when they worked together on the construction of a house for Wittgenstein's sister.

In addition to Olmütz and Tel Aviv there was one other town which played a prominent part in his life: Vienna, where he studied architecture under Adolf Loos, and where he saw a lot of Karl Kraus and Ludwig Wittgenstein.

Engelmann's work as an architect excels in both beauty and simplicity of form. He did not, however, turn his reputation as an architect into financial gain, but confined this activity to the minimum indispensable for his needs, so as to have time to spare for his intellectual pursuits. His unpublished writings include a work on psychology in graphic presentation. He also edited a series of publications on problems of art and philosophy and on figures such as Adolf Loos and Karl Kraus.

It was Engelmann's endeavour to influence his human

environment. He did not only intend to change the interior of habitations, but also meant to reform town planning, the economy, and intellectual life as a whole. His influence, however, remained limited. His life is summed up in what Karl Kraus says in the poem below about the runner who comes from the origin:

TWO RUNNERS

Two runners run the track of time,
Reckless the one, the other strides in awe.
The one, from nowhere, wins his goal; the other —
The origin his start — dies on the way.
And he from nowhere, he that won, yields place
To him who ever strides in awe and e'er
Has reached his terminus: the origin.

Engelmann was a mystic in Wittgenstein's sense. To him the meaning of the world and the purpose of life lay outside the physical and psychological universe. At the same time his cultural-philosophical investigations and his writings on psychology, like his economic and town-planning projects, are entirely based on rational argument, since the mystic element can only become manifest but never be communicated in explicit statements.

Engelmann wrote poetry both in his youth and later in life. One of his poems is referred to in a letter by Ludwig Wittgenstein published in this book (No. *8*). Engelmann's posthumous papers also include a voluminous anthology of four centuries of German literature. We must hope that it will be possible to publish his writings.

Haifa, May 1965.   Josef Schächter

Editor's Note

This book ought not to appear without some tribute to Paul Engelmann's devoted friends, Dr. Josef Schächter, Dr. Max Zweig, and Mr. Shimshon Stein, who have made its publication possible. Mr. Stein assembled the materials from Engelmann's papers and prepared the German typescript with exemplary care.

The original letters from Wittgenstein have been consulted for the present edition and in the spelling and punctuation of the German their practice has been followed. Apart from that, my own responsibility extends to the correction of one or two errors of fact, the footnotes, the appendix, and the spelling and punctuation of the English. It has been a pleasure to work with the translator, Dr. Furtmüller. I am grateful also to Mr. John Hevesi, who put me in touch with Engelmann and thus made the material here presented and the *Tractatus* typescript available to a wider public.

Wittgenstein's literary executors (Miss Elizabeth Anscombe, Mr. Rush Rhees, and Professor G. H. von Wright) have generously permitted the publication of the letters. Miss Anscombe is referred to in Engelmann's 'Introduction'. Professor von Wright too gave encouragement to Engelmann and he has been of great help to me.

I share the deep regret of Engelmann's friends that he did not live to bring this work to a more complete form or to see its publication.

January 1967.   B. F. McG.

Introduction

In the years which have passed since Wittgenstein became famous I have received many suggestions and proposals that I should at last publish these letters. One of the reasons why I have not done so has been the fact that, although I am of course identical with the person to whom these letters were addressed, it is equally true to say in the words of the popular phrase that since that time 'I have become a completely different person'. This is not only due to the great difference – in my case particularly marked – between the attitudes of youth and of old age. The very traits in my character which caused Wittgenstein to choose my company at all, and made him talk and write to me as he did, have changed a great deal, although obviously some things have remained constant.

It will be appreciated, therefore, that the judgement which Wittgenstein expressed at the time about my person, character, and abilities – undoubtedly too favourable a judgement in some respects – is today a source of some embarrassment to me, especially when I think that readers who do not know me personally might automatically apply this assessment to the recipient of the letters as he is today. All these negative considerations are still valid as far as I am concerned, but external circumstances have vastly changed in recent years.

Posthumous fame is like the satyric drama following the tragedy of a life of genius. It was the peculiar manifestations of that kind of fame which induced me in 1958 to write at some length to Miss Elizabeth Anscombe, whom I knew by name not only as the Editor of the *Philosophical Investigations* but also as a pupil of Wittgenstein's who was close to him during the last years of his life. I said in the course of my letter that I was not particularly keen on writing down and publishing my reminiscences of Wittgenstein; he would surely have been annoyed to find that some parts of his private intellectual life which he had seen fit to communicate in a specific form to one intimate acquaintance were now being passed on to a wider literary and philosophic public which, I know, he held – rightly, on the whole – in poor esteem. This, indeed, was why – quite apart from my personal objections – I felt under no obligation to publish my material, even though it might have led to a desirable and important rectification of the accepted account of Wittgenstein's views. I asked Miss Anscombe's advice, and she wrote in her reply:

If by pressing a button it could have been secured that people would not concern themselves with his personal life, I should have pressed the button; but since that has not been possible and it is certain that much that is foolish will keep on being said, it seems to me reasonable that anyone who can write a truthful account of him should do so. On the other hand to write a satisfactory account would seem to need extraordinary talent. — Further, I must confess that I feel deeply suspicious of anyone's claim to have understood Wittgenstein. That is perhaps because, although I had a very strong and deep affection for him, and, I suppose, knew him well, I am very sure that I did not understand him. It is difficult, I think, not to give a version of his attitudes, for example, which one can enter into oneself, and then the account is really of oneself: is for example infected with one's own mediocrity or ordinariness or lack of complexity. . . .

This on the whole encouraging reply was one of the reasons which eventually induced me to compile this book in its present form. Unfortunately, however, I have not been able to live up to Miss Anscombe's expectation that I could present an objective picture of Wittgenstein's personality. Nevertheless she has kindly granted me the copyright of the letters presented here – which is vested in her and her co-executors – and my heartfelt thanks are due to her for this kindness. I am aware that it is far beyond my literary gifts to present an objective picture of Wittgenstein's personality. The picture which my disposition enables me to give is entirely subjective, comparable to the likeness of an eminent man presented by a good portrait painter. Accordingly it is not false modesty if I accept that 'my account is really only of myself; infected with my own mediocrity or ordinariness or lack of complexity' – in fact, with all three.

Since I received this letter the faithful account of Wittgenstein's life by Norman Malcolm and Georg Henrik von Wright has been published. It proves that it is perfectly possible to present an objective yet vivid picture of so complex a man as Wittgenstein, though this is not the task for me. On the other hand, there is one, and only one, period in Wittgenstein's life that is not touched upon in that account and this is precisely the period in which the letters here presented were written, the period of the preparation and publication of the *Tractatus*. This is one justification for bringing out this book. Whether it remains the only justification for what I have to give will depend on whether I have suceeded in illuminating his life through mine as well as mine through his.

Tel Aviv, January 1965.

I. *Letters from Wittgenstein*

I. *Briefe von Wittgenstein*

Lieber Herr Engelmann! 25.12.16

Heute auf einen Sprung bei Loos. Er ist noch immer nicht zum Arbeiten gekommen, sagt aber, Sie werden die Zeichnungen binnen 14 Tagen erhalten. Ich aber schwöre darauf, daß diese Arbeit auch nicht wird *angefangen* werden! Schreiben Sie mir wie es Ihnen geht, und was Sie treiben. Denken Sie an mich und empfehlen Sie mich Ihren Herrn Eltern. Ihr ergebener

Ludw Wittgenstein

2

Lieber Herr Engelmann! 4.1.17

Loos ist nicht in Wien. Er fuhr am 25.12. nach Tirol und wollte gestern (3.1.) zurückkommen. Er wird also wahrscheinlich Samstag schon hier sein. Ich fahre Samstag abends ab und kann Sie daher nicht mehr sehen. – Fritz Zweig war bei mir.

Ich gehe wahrscheinlich in kürzester Zeit ins Feld zurück. Möge es uns allen gut gehen!

Herzlichste Grüße an Sie und die Ihren.

Ludw Wittgenstein

3

[Feldpostkarte] [Poststempel 26.1.17]

Kann wieder arbeiten, Gott sei Dank! Schreiben Sie mir gleich und ausführlich, wie es Ihnen geht. Grüßen Sie Alle herzlichst und sich selbst auch.

Wittgenstein

I. *Letters from Wittgenstein*[1]

1

Dear Mr. Engelmann,   25.12.16

Called briefly on Loos today.[2] He still has not got down to the work, but says you will get the drawings within a fortnight. I myself, though, am prepared to swear that the work will not even be *started*.

Let me know how you are getting on and what you are doing. Think of me and give my respects to your parents.[3]

Yours sincerely
Ludw Wittgenstein

2

Dear Mr. Engelmann,   4.1.17

Loos is not in Vienna. He left on 25.12 for the Tyrol and meant to return yesterday (3.1). So he will probably be here by Saturday. I shall leave here Saturday night and therefore shall not be able to see you. – I have had a visit from Fritz Zweig.[4]

I shall probably return very soon to the front. May things go well with all of us!

Kindest regards to you and your family.

Ludw Wittgenstein

3

[Field-postcard]   [Postmark 26.1.17]

I can work again, thank God! Write quickly and in detail how you are. Give my regards to everybody, including yourself.

Wittgenstein

---

[1] The figures given in the footnotes refer to the chapter and section of the text where further explanation will be found. Dates in brackets have been added by the recipient.

[2] II. 3, VII. 3.   [3] II. 2.   [4] II. 4.

[Feldpostkarte]   29.3.17

Möchte Ihnen auch bald ausführlich schreiben. Ich
denke oft mit Freude an Sie. Herzliche Grüße.

L Wittgenstein

Lieber Herr Engelmann!   31.3.17

Ich habe zwei Ursachen Ihnen heute zu schreiben. Die
erste will ich Ihnen später sagen, die zweite ist, daß jemand
von hier nach Olmütz fährt. Die Erste ist folgende:
Ich erhielt heute aus Zürich zwei Bücher jenes Albert
Ehrenstein, der seinerzeit in *Die Fackel* schrieb (Ich habe
ihn einmal ohne es eigentlich zu wollen unterstützt) und
zum Dank schickt er mir jetzt den *Tubutsch* und *Der Mensch
schreit*. Ein Hundedreck; wenn ich mich nicht irre. Und so
etwas bekomme ich hier heraus! Bitte schicken Sie mir –
als Gegengift – Goethes Gedichte, *zweiter Band*, wo die
venetianischen Epigramme die Elegien und Episteln
stehen! Und auch noch die Gedichte von Mörike
(Reklam)! Ich arbeite ziemlich fleißig und wollte, ich
wäre besser und gescheidter. Und diese beiden sind ein
und dasselbe. – Gott helfe mir! Ich denke oft an Sie. An
den *Sommernachtstraum* und an das zweite Ballett im
Eingebildeten Kranken, und daran, daß Sie mir Suppe gebracht
haben. Aber daran ist auch Ihre Frau Mama schuld,
die mir auch unvergeßlich ist. Bitte empfehlen Sie mich
ihr. – Grüßen Sie Zweig und Groag.

Ihr

L. Wittgenstein

Grüßen Sie bitte auch Herrn Lachs von mir.

[Field-postcard]   29.3.17

I should also like to write to you soon and at length.
I think of you often and with true pleasure. Kind regards.

L Wittgenstein

5

Dear Mr. Engelmann,   31.3.17

I have two reasons for writing to you today. The first I
will tell you later; the second is that someone is going to
Olmütz from here.[1] The first reason is this: I received
today from Zurich two books by Albert Ehrenstein[2] – the
one who used to write in *Die Fackel*[3] (once I helped him
financially without really wanting to). Now he returns the
favour by sending me his *Tubutsch* and *Man Screams*. It's
just muck if I am not mistaken. And such stuff is sent to
me out here! Please send me, as an antidote, Goethe's
poems, the *second volume*, which has the Venetian Epigrams,
the Elegies, and the Epistles![2] Also Mörike's poems[2]
(Reclam edition). I am working reasonably hard and wish
I were a better man and had a better mind. These two
things are really one and the same. – God help me! I
often think of you, of the *Midsummer Night's Dream* and
the second ballet in the *Malade Imaginaire*,[4] and of the
time when you brought me some soup. But that was your
mother's fault as well as yours! And I shall never forget
her either. Please give her my respects. – Remember me
to Zweig and Groag.[5]

Yours
L. Wittgenstein

Please remember me also to Mr. Lachs.

[1] II. 1.
[2] IV. 2 and Appendix.
[3] The journal published by Karl Kraus in Vienna.
[4] II. 6.
[5] II. 4.

Lieber Herr Engelmann! 9.4.17
    Vielen Dank für Ihren lieben Brief und die Bücher. Das Uhlandsche Gedicht ist wirklich großartig. Und es ist so: Wenn man sich nicht bemüht das Unaussprechliche auszusprechen, so geht *nichts* verloren. Sondern das Unaussprechliche ist, – unaussprechlich – in dem Ausgesprochenen *enthalten*!
    Die Händel-Variationen von Brahms kenne ich. Unheimlich –
    Was Ihre wechselnde Stimmung betrifft so ist es so: Wir schlafen. (Ich habe das schon einmal Herrn Groag gesagt, und es ist wahr.) *Unser* Leben ist wie ein Traum. In den besseren Stunden aber wachen wir so weit auf daß wir erkennen daß wir träumen. Meistens sind wir aber im Tiefschlaf. Ich kann mich nicht selber aufwecken! Ich bemühe mich, mein Traumleib macht Bewegungen, aber mein wirklicher *rührt sich nicht*. So ist es leider!
Ihr
Wittgenstein

7

[Feldpostkarte] [Poststempel 27.8.(17)]
    Ich danke Ihnen für Ihre Karte. Ich hätte Ihnen viel mitzuteilen kann aber nichts schreiben. Mein Gehirn arbeitet sehr kräftig. Empfehlen Sie mich wärmstens Ihrer Frau Mutter.
    Sein Sie herzlich gegrüßt.
Wittgenstein

8

L. H. E.! [Ohne Datum]
    Bitte sagen Sie Herrn Groag er möchte trotz der Gefahr so lieb sein, und mir meine Manuskripte schicken. Wenn sie dann verloren gehen so war es Gottes Wille.
    Ferners, bitte, schicken Sie mir eine Abschrift Ihres

Dear Mr. Engelmann, 9.4.17

Many thanks for your kind letter and the books. The poem by Uhland[1] is really magnificent. And this is how it is: if only you do not try to utter what is unutterable then *nothing* gets lost. But the unutterable will be – unutterably – *contained* in what has been uttered!

As for Brahms's Handel Variations – I do know them. Uncanny –

About your changeable mood: it is like this: We are asleep. (I have said this once before to Mr. Groag, and it is true.) *Our* life is like a dream. But in our better hours we wake up just enough to realise that we are dreaming. Most of the time, though, we are fast asleep. I cannot awaken myself! I am trying hard, my dream body moves, but my real one *does not stir*. This, alas, is how it is!

Yours
Wittgenstein

7

[Field-postcard] [Postmark 27.8.(17)]

Thank you for your card. I have a lot to tell you but cannot write. My brain is working very vigorously. Give my respects and warmest greetings to your mother.

Kind regards to you.

Wittgenstein

8

D. Mr. E., [Undated]

Please tell Mr. Groag to be kind enough to send me my manuscripts, in spite of the danger. If they do get lost, it was God's will.

[1] IV. 1.

Gedichtes. Ich werde sie nicht mißbrauchen und das Gedicht nur meiner Schwester Mining vorlesen. Ich wäre Ihnen sehr dankbar. Ich habe mich *sehr* gefreut Sie gesehen und gesprochen zu haben. Es hat mich *erfrischt*. Bitte emfehlen Sie mich Ihrer verehrten, lieben Frau Mutter.

Ihr L. Wittgenstein

9

L. H. E.!

4.9.17

   Bitte sein Sie so gut und schicken Sie mir die Bibel in einem kleinen aber noch leserlichen Format. Meine Adresse ist: F.H.R. 5/4 Feldp. 286. Ich hätte Ihnen manches mitzuteilen, kann es aber noch immer nicht herausgeben.

   Möchte es Ihnen gut gehen. Ich denke oft an Sie.

Beste Grüße
L Wittgenstein

10

[Feldpostkarte]

4.10.17

   Besten Dank für die Bücher. Herzliche Grüße.

Wittgenstein

11

L. H. E.!

28.10.17

   Mit Freude habe ich gehört daß Sie in Neuwaldegg alles auf den Kopf stellen. Auch meine liebe Mama hat einen Narren an Ihnen gefressen, was ich übrigens vollkommen verstehe. Ich arbeite ziemlich viel bin aber trotzdem unruhig. Möchten Sie so anständig bleiben als es gern wäre

Ihr L. Wittgenstein.

Furthermore, please send me a copy of your poem.[1] I shall not misuse it and will read the poem only to my sister Mining. I should be very grateful to you. I was *very* glad to have seen you and talked to you. It has *refreshed* me. Please give my respects to your revered dear mother.

Yours L. Wittgenstein

9

D. Mr. E.,   4.9.17
Please be kind enough to send me the Bible in a small-size but still legible edition. My address is F.H.R. 5/4 Field-Post 286. There are quite a number of things I have to tell you, but I still cannot let them out.

May things go well with you. I often think of you.

Kind regards
L Wittgenstein

10

[Field-postcard]   4.10.17
Many thanks for the books. Kind regards.

Wittgenstein

11

D. Mr. E.,   28.10.17
I was pleased to hear that you are turning everything upside down at Neuwaldegg.[2] My dear Mama, too, has a very soft spot for you – which, by the way, I perfectly understand. I work a fair amount but am restless all the same. May you remain as decent as would love to be

Yours L. Wittgenstein

[1] III. 2.
[2] A district on the outskirts of Vienna where the Wittgensteins had a spring and autumn house.

9

Lieber Freund! 16.1.18

Besten Dank für Ihre Zeilen vom 8./1. Wenn ich sie
nur verstünde! Aber ich verstehe sie nicht. Es ist allerdings
ein Unterschied zwischen mir jetzt und damals, als wir
uns in Olmütz sahen. Und dieser Unterschied ist soviel ich
weiß der, daß ich jetzt *ein wenig* anständiger bin. Damit
meine ich nur daß ich mir jetzt ein wenig klarer über meine
Unanständigkeit bin als damals. Wenn Sie nun sagen daß
ich keinen Glauben habe, so haben Sie *ganz recht,* nur hatte
ich ihn auch früher nicht. Es ist ja klar, daß der Mensch
der, so zu sagen, eine Maschine erfinden will um anständig
zu werden, daß dieser Mensch keinen Glauben hat. Aber
was soll ich tun? *Das eine ist mir klar:* Ich bin viel zu
schlecht um über mich spintisieren zu können, sondern, ich
werde entweder ein Schweinehund bleiben oder mich
bessern, und damit basta! Nur kein transzendentales
Geschwätz, wenn alles so klar ist wie eine Watschen.

Es ist nicht unmöglich daß ich bald nach Olmütz zum
Kader komme!

Sie haben gewiß in allem ganz recht.

Denken Sie an Ihren
ergebenen
L. Wittgenstein

L. H. E.! 9.4.18

Eine große Bitte: Als ich damals in Olmütz den
Darmkatarrh hatte verschrieb mir Dr. Hahn eine Medizin,
die *einzige* welche mir je genützt hat. Nun habe ich das
Rezept verloren, aber den Katarrh leider nicht. Möchten
Sie die große Güte haben zu Dr. Hahn zu gehen und ihn
zu bitten mir das Rezept noch einmal auszustellen;
wenn er nämlich die Medizin nach ihrer äußeren Beschrei-
bung erkennt – denn was darin war weiß ich nicht. Es

Dear friend, 16.1.18

Many thanks for your letter of 8.1. If only I understood it! But I do not understand it. It is true there is a difference between myself as I am now and as I was when we met in Olmütz. And, as far as I know, the difference is that I am now *slightly* more decent. By this I only mean that I am slightly clearer in my own mind about my lack of decency. If you tell me now that I have no faith, you are *perfectly right*, only I did not have it before either. It is plain, isn't it, that when a man wants, as it were, to invent a machine for becoming decent, such a man has no faith. But what am I to do? *I am clear about one thing:* I am far too bad to be able to theorize about myself; in fact I shall either remain a swine or else I shall improve, and that's that! Only let's cut out the transcendental twaddle when the whole thing is as plain as a sock on the jaw.

It is not impossible that I may soon be transferred to Olmütz!

I am sure you are quite right in all you say.

Think of
Yours sincerely
L. Wittgenstein

D. Mr. E., 9.4.18

A big request: When I was down with enteritis in Olmütz, Dr. Hahn prescribed some medicine for me, the *only one* that has ever helped me. Now I have lost the prescription, but unfortunately not the enteritis. Could you be so very kind as to go to Dr. Hahn and beg him to write out the prescription again? Provided, that is, he recognizes the medicine from an external description – because I don't know what was in it. It was a turbid

war eine trübe etwas gelbliche Flüssigkeit auf deren Grund
ein weißer Satz war, den man aufschütteln mußte worauf
die Flüssigkeit wie Milch aussah. Geschmack süßlich und
angenehm; (jeden Tag 2 Eßlöffel). Wenn er mir das R.
noch einmal ausstellen kann, dann, bitte, sein Sie so
lieb, es mir zu schicken. Meine Adresse ist: *Geb. Kan. Btt.
5/11, Feldp. 290*
    Ich denke oft und mit Freude an Sie. Bitte empfehlen
Sie mich Ihrer verehrten Frau Mutter.

Ihr
L Wittgenstein

14

[Feldpostkarte]   1.6.18
    Schicke Ihnen ein paar Bücher, die Sie nicht verdienen,
da Sie sogar zu faul sind auf eine dringende Anfrage zu
antworten.

Wittgenstein

15

[Ansichtskarte aus Salzburg]   14.7.18
    Werde wahrscheinlich bald nach Wien kommen. Besten
Gruß.

Wittgenstein

16

[Feldpostkarte]   9.10.18
    Warum ich Ihnen schreibe, weiß ich selbst nicht. Teils
aus langer Weile, teils weil alles mögliche in mir ist, was
ich gerne schriebe, aber nicht schreiben kann. Mit Freuden
erinnere ich mich an unsere Zeit auf der Hochreit. Mein
Leben ist eigentlich sehr glücklich! Bis auf die Zeiten wo

yellowish liquid with a white sediment at the bottom, which you had to shake up, when the liquid turned milky. Taste: sweetish and pleasant; (two tablespoons daily). If he can write out the prescription again, please do me a favour and send it on to me. My address is: *Mountain Artillery Battery 5/11, Field-post 290.*

I think of you often and with true pleasure. Please give my respects to your revered mother.

Yours

L Wittgenstein

14

[Field-postcard]   1.6.18

Am sending you a few books which you don't deserve as you are too lazy even to answer an urgent inquiry.

Wittgenstein

15

[Picture postcard from Salzburg]   14.7.18

Shall probably come to Vienna soon. Kind regards.

Wittgenstein

16

[Field-postcard]   9.10.18

Why I am writing to you I do not know myself. Partly out of boredom, partly because I have a lot of things inside me which I would like to write but cannot. I remember with much pleasure our stay together on the Hochreit.[1] Come to that, I have a very happy life! Except when it is

[1] An estate in Lower Austria where Wittgenstein's father had built houses for his family to use in the summer.

es verflucht unglücklich ist. (Das ist kein Witz). Jahoda
hat noch immer nicht geruht mir sein Urteil zu schreiben.
Ich bin schon sehr gespannt.

Ihr alter
Wittgenstein

17

[Feldpostkarte]   22.10.18
L. H. E.! Noch immer habe ich keine Antwort vom
Verleger erhalten! Und ich habe eine unüberwindliche
Abneigung dagegen, ihm zu schreiben und anzufragen.
Weiß der Teufel, was er mit meinem Manuskript treibt.
Vielleicht untersucht er es chemisch auf seine Tauglichkeit.
Bitte haben Sie die *große* Güte und machen Sie einmal,
wenn Sie in Wien sind, einen Sprung zu dem verfluchten
Kujon und schreiben mir dann das Ergebnis! Zum
Arbeiten komme ich jetzt nicht, aber vielleicht zum
Krepieren.

Ihr alter
Wittgenstein

18

25.10.18
L. H. E.! Heute erhielt ich von Jahoda die Mitteilung,
daß er meine Arbeit nicht drucken kann. Angeblich aus
technischen Gründen. Ich wüßte aber gar zu gern, was
Kraus zu ihr gesagt hat. Wenn Sie Gelegenheit hätten es zu
erfahren, so würde ich mich sehr freuen. Vielleicht weiß
Loos etwas. Schreiben Sie mir.

Ihr
Wittgenstein

damned unhappy (this is not a joke). Jahoda[1] has still not condescended to give me his judgement. So I am waiting with bated breath.

Ever yours
Wittgenstein

17

[Field-postcard]   22.10.18

D. Mr. E., – Still no reply from the publisher! And I feel an insuperable repugnance against writing to him with a query. The devil knows what he is doing with my manuscript. Perhaps he is examining it chemically as to its fitness. Please be so *very* kind and look up the damned blighter some day when you are in Vienna, and then let me know the result! I get no time to work these days, though possibly enough, to cop it.

Ever yours
Wittgenstein

18

25.10.18

D. Mr. E., – Today I received notification from Jahoda that he cannot publish my treatise. Allegedly for technical reasons. But I would dearly like to know what Kraus[2] said about it. If there were an opportunity for you to find out, I should be very glad. Perhaps Loos knows something about it. Do write to me.

Yours
Wittgenstein

[1] A Viennese publisher who published *Die Fackel*.
[2] VII. 2.

[Karte aus der ital. Kriegsgefangenschaft.
Absender: Ludwig Wittgenstein, Sottotenente,
Cassino, Prov. Caserta]   24.5.19
   Besten Dank für Ihre liebe Karte vom 3./4. und für die
günstige Rezension. Ich mache jetzt schwere Zeiten in
meinem Inneren durch! Viel hätte auch ich zu sagen! –
Nun eine Bitte: Schicken Sie mir, bitte, womöglich sicher
und rasch, die *Grundgesetze* von Frege hierher. Es wird schon
irgendwie gehen. Möchte es Ihnen gut gehen.
                              Herzlichste Grüße
                              Ihr Wittgenstein

                              20
Lieber Herr Engelmann!   Wien, 25.8.19
   Wie Sie sehen, bin ich hier! Ich hätte unendlich viel
mit Ihnen zu besprechen. Es geht mir nicht sehr gut (nämlich geistig). Kommen Sie womöglich bald zu mir. Grüßen
Sie, bitte, Ihre verehrte Frau Mutter herzlichst und erge-
benst von mir.
                              Auf Wiedersehen!
                              Ihr Wittgenstein

                              21
Lieber Herr Engelmann!   2.9.19
   Vielen Dank für Ihren Brief. Nach Olmütz kann ich in
der nächsten Zeit nicht kommen. Ich fahre morgen auf
die Hochreit für 8–10 Tage, um mich womöglich ein
bißchen wieder zu finden. Und nachher ergreife ich einen
Beruf! Welchen? Sie haben Zeit zu raten bis Sie zu mir
kommen. – Vor ein paar Tagen besuchte ich Loos. Ich
war entsetzt und angeekelt. Er ist bis zur Unmöglichkeit
verschmockt! Er gab mir eine Brochure über ein geplantes

[Postcard from Italian prisoner-of-
war camp. Sender: Ludwig
Wittgenstein, Sottotenente, Cassino,
Prov. Caserta]   24.5.19

Many thanks for your kind postcard of 3.4 and for the
favourable review. I am going through hard times men-
tally! I, too, have a lot to say! Now a request: please send
me, safely and quickly if you can, Frege's *Grundgesetze*.[1]
You will manage it somehow, I am sure. May things go
well with you.

Kindest regards
Yours Wittgenstein

Dear Mr. Engelmann,   Vienna, 25.8.19

As you see I am here! There is no end of things I want to
talk to you about. I am not very well (i.e. as far as my state
of mind is concerned). Come to me soon, if you can. Please
give my sincere and humble regards to your revered
mother.

Auf Wiedersehen!
Yours Wittgenstein

Dear Mr. Engelmann,   2.9.19

Many thanks for your letter. I cannot come to Olmütz
in the near future. Tomorrow I will go to the Hochreit
for 8–10 days, to find something of myself again if I can.
And after that I shall embark on a career. What career?
You have time to guess till you come and visit me. – A few
days ago I looked up Loos. I was horrified and nauseated.
He has become infected with the most virulent bogus
intellectualism! He gave me a pamphlet about a proposed

---

[1] *Grundgesetze der Arithmetik*, 1893–1903, now available in translation as *The Basic Laws of Arithmetic*.

'Kunstamt', wo er über die Sünde wider den Heiligen Geist spricht. Da hört sich alles auf! Ich kam in sehr gedrückter Stimmung zu ihm und das hatte mir gerade noch gefehlt. *Viel, viel,* hätte ich mit Ihnen zu besprechen. Vor ein paar Tagen habe ich eine Kopie meiner Arbeit dem Braumüller zum Verlegen gegeben. Er hat sich aber noch nicht entschieden, ob er sie nehmen will.

Bitte danken Sie Ihrer Frau Mutter herzlichst für ihre lieben Zeilen. Ich freue mich *sehr* auf ein baldiges Wiedersehen!

Ihr Ludwig Wittgenstein

22

25.9.19

L. H. E.! Vor einigen Tagen schrieb mir Max Zweig, daß er mich in der nächsten Zeit in Olmütz erwartet. Er hat also aus meinem Schreiben an Sie das Gegenteil von dem entnommen, was darin stand. Und vielleicht Sie auch! – Ich kann aber tatsächlich nicht kommen, weil ich einen Beruf ergriffen habe (es war kein Witz). Sie brauchen aber nicht mehr zu raten, da die Sache schon perfekt ist. Ich gehe in die Lehrerbildungsanstalt, um Lehrer zu werden. Ich sitze also wieder in einer Schule; und das klingt komischer als es ist. Es fällt mir nämlich ungemein schwer; ich kann mich nicht mehr so benehmen wie ein Mittelschüler, und – so komisch es klingt – die Demütigung ist für mich eine *so* große, daß ich sie oft kaum ertragen zu können glaube! Nun, von einer Fahrt nach Olmütz ist also keine Rede. Aber wie gerne möchte ich Sie sehen! Wenn *irgend* möglich, so kommen Sie, bitte, nach Wien! Schreiben Sie gleich. Meine Adresse ist: III. Untere Viaduktgasse 9, bei Frau Wonicek. (Es haben sich nämlich auch meine übrigen Verhältnisse geändert – gescheiter bin ich aber nicht geworden.)

Ihr L. Wittgenstein

Bitte empfehlen Sie mich Ihrer Frau Mama.

'fine arts office', in which he speaks about a sin against the Holy Ghost.[1] This surely is the limit! I was already a bit depressed when I went to Loos, but that was the last straw! There is *very much* I want to talk to you about. A few days ago I gave Braumüller[2] a copy of my treatise for publication. But he has not yet made up his mind whether he will accept it.

Please give your mother my sincere thanks for her kind lines to me. I am *much* looking forward to seeing you again soon! Yours Ludwig Wittgenstein

22

25.9.19

D. Mr. E., – A few days ago Max Zweig[3] wrote to me that he was expecting me shortly in Olmütz. So he gathered from my letter to you exactly the opposite of what it said. And perhaps you did, too!—But I really cannot come, because I have taken up a career (I was not pulling your leg). I won't keep you guessing any more, as the matter is now finally settled. I am attending a teachers' training college in order to become a schoolmaster. So once again I sit in a schoolroom, and this sounds funnier than it is. In fact I find it terribly hard; I can no longer behave like a grammar-school boy, and – funny as it sounds – the humiliation is *so* great for me that often I think I can hardly bear it! Well, a trip to Olmütz is out of the question now. But how much I want to see you! If *at all* possible, please do come to Vienna! Write at once. My address is III. Untere Viaduktgasse 9, c/o Frau Wonicek. (In fact, my circumstances have changed in general, except that I am no wiser than I was.) Yours L. Wittgenstein

Please give my respects to your Mama.

[1] In 'Der Staat und die Kunst', Loos's preface to *richtlinien für ein kunstamt*, 1919 (*Sämtliche Schriften*, I, Vienna 1962, pp. 352–4). It is a sin against the Holy Ghost for the State, as opposed to an individual, to fail to recognize a true artist.
[2] The publisher of Otto Weininger. [3] II. 4.

16.11.19

L. H. E.! Vor wenigen Tagen erhielt ich Ihren Brief.
Vielen Dank! Ihren Zustand glaube ich ganz zu verstehen.
Denn ich befinde mich gerade jetzt in einem ähnlichen
und zwar schon seit meiner Rückkehr aus der Gefangen-
schaft. Ich glaube es geht damit *so* zu: Wir gehen nicht
auf der direkten Straße zum Ziel, dazu haben wir – oder
ich wenigstens – nicht die Kraft. Dagegen gehen wir auf
allen möglichen Seitenwegen und so lange wir auf einem
solchen vorwärtskommen, geht es uns so leidlich. Wie
aber ein solcher Weg aufhört, so stehen wir da und werden
uns nun erst bewußt, daß wir ja nicht dort sind, wo wir
hingehören. – So wenigstens kommt mir die Sache vor. –
Ich habe ein großes Bedürfnis Sie zu sehen und zu sprechen.
Wie weit ich heruntergekommen bin, ersehen Sie daraus,
daß ich schon einige Male daran gedacht habe, mir das
Leben zu nehmen, aber nicht etwa aus Verzweiflung
über meine Schlechtigkeit, sondern aus ganz äußerlichen
Gründen. Ob ein Gespräch mit Ihnen mir etwas helfen
würde, ist zwar zweifelhaft, aber doch nicht ausgeschlossen.
Also kommen Sie bald.

Ihr
Ludwig Wittgenstein

Meine Adresse ist jetzt:
XIII. St. Veitgasse 17
bei Frau Sjögren

Die normalen Menschen sind mir eine Wohltat, und eine
Qual zugleich.

Lieber Herr Engelmann! 27.11.19
Da ich jeden Vormittag in der Stadt in die Schule
gehe und Sie am besten mittags und abends in der Alleegasse bei meiner Mama essen, so nehme ich Ihnen kein

16.11.19

D. Mr. E., – I got your letter a few days ago. Many
thanks! I think I entirely understand your state of mind.
My own, in fact, is very similar, and has been so since my
return from prison camp. What happens, I believe, is this:
we do not advance towards our goal by the direct road –
for this we (or at any rate I) have not got the strength.
Instead we walk up all sorts of tracks and byways, and so
long as we are making some headway we are in reasonably
good shape. But whenever such a track comes to an end
we are up against it; only then do we realise that we are
not at all where we ought to be. – This, at least, is how the
matter looks to me. – I have a great urge to see you and
speak to you. Just how far I have gone downhill you can
see from the fact that I have on several occasions contem-
plated taking my own life. Not from my despair about my
own badness but for purely external reasons. Whether a
talk with you would help me to some extent is doubtful,
but not impossible.

So come soon.

Yours
Ludwig Wittgenstein

My present address is:
 XIII. St. Veitgasse 17
 c/o Frau Sjögren

Normal human beings are a balm to me, and a torment at
the same time.

Dear Mr. Engelmann,   27.11.19
 As I have to go to school in town every morning and
it will be best for you to eat at lunch time and in the
evening at my Mama's in the Alleegasse, I will not take

Zimmer in Hietzing, sondern eines im IV. Bezirk. Wo,
daß weiß ich jetzt noch nicht und darum kommen Sie von
der Bahn direkt zu uns (in die Allegasse), wo Sie alles
nähere erfahren werden. – Für heute nur noch so viel,
daß ich mich sehr auf Sie freue und daß ich Scherereien mit
meinem Buch habe die mich gar nicht freuen.

Ihr
Ludwig Wittgenstein

25

N. V. Vegetarisch Hotel-Restaurant
'Pomona'
Molenstraat 53   Den Haag   Den Haag, 15.12.19
L. H. E.! Wie Sie sehen bin ich hier in einem Tugend-
bündlerhotel. Es geht mir sehr gut. Russell will meine
Abhandlung drucken und zwar vielleicht deutsch und
englisch (er wird sie selbst übersetzen und eine Einleitung
zu ihr schreiben, was mir ganz recht ist). Eigentlich wollte
ich Ihnen aber nur darum schreiben, um Ihnen zu sagen
daß es mich ungemein gefreut hat, mit Ihnen gesprochen
zu haben. Aber sehr schade, daß es so kurz war! Ich hätte
noch vieles zu besprechen gehabt. Oder vielmehr das *Eine*
noch gründlicher, denn ich kenne mich noch immer nicht
aus. Grüßen Sie Ihre verehrte Frau Mama gehorsamst von
mir.

Ihr
Ludwig Wittgenstein

Besten Gruß
Arvid Sjögren

a room for you in Hietzing but in the IVth District.[1] I don't know yet where; so come straight from the station to us (in the Alleegasse), where you will be told all further details. – I will only add that I am looking forward with joy to your coming, and that I have troubles with my book which give me no joy at all.

Yours
Ludwig Wittgenstein

25

N. V. Vegetarisch Hotel-Restaurant
          'Pomona'
Molenstraat 53   Den Haag   The Hague, 15.12.19
D. Mr. E., – As you see I am here at a place for the promotion of virtue. I am getting on very well. Russell wants to print my treatise, possibly in both German and English (he will translate it himself and write an introduction, which suits me). Actually I meant to write to you only in order to tell you that I was extremely glad to have talked to you. What a pity, though, that it was so short! I had a lot more to discuss. Or rather, just the *one* matter but that still more thoroughly, because I still do not understand it all. Give my humble regards to your revered Mama.

Yours
Ludwig Wittgenstein

Kind regards
Arvid Sjögren[2]

[1] Hietzing is the XIIIth District where Wittgenstein at that time lived. The town house of his family was a large house in the Argentinierstrasse (formerly Alleegasse) in the IVth District, see Chapter VI.

[2] Mr. Sjögren, a friend of Wittgenstein's and the son of his landlady at the time, accompanied him to Holland as later to Norway (cf. letter *41*).

29.12.19

L. H. E.! Bin vorgestern aus Holland zurückgekommen.
Mein Zusammensein mit Russell war sehr genußreich.
Er will eine Einleitung zu meinem Buch schreiben und ich
habe mich damit einverstanden erklärt. Ich möchte nun
noch einmal versuchen einen Verleger dafür zu gewinnen.
Mit einer Einleitung von Russell ist das Buch für einen
Verleger gewiß ein sehr geringes Risiko da Russell sehr
bekannt ist. Vielleicht schreiben Sie dem Herrn der mich
Reklam empfehlen soll in diesem Sinne. Falls ich keinen
deutschen Verleger finden kann so wird Russell das Buch
in England drucken lassen. Da er in diesem Falle alle
möglichen Schritte zu unternehmen hätte so bitte ich
Sie mir so bald als irgend möglich Bescheid zu geben ob
Ihre Bemühungen irgendwelchen Erfolg versprechen. – – –
Meine Stimmung ist jetzt sehr gedrückt. Mein Verhältnis
zu meinen Nebenmenschen hat sich auf eine eigenthüm-
liche Art verändert. Das was in Ordnung war als wir uns
sahen ist jetzt in Unordnung und ich bin in einer richtigen
Verzweiflung. Ich sehe übrigens voraus daß es ziemlich
lange branchen wird ehe etwas entscheidendes geschieht.
Wie gerne würde ich Sie bald wiedersehen: Denn in der
Betätigung meines Verstandes die Sie mir ermöglichen liegt
für mich doch eine gewisse Beruhigung. – Empfehlen Sie
mich herzlichst Ihrer Frau Mama. –
                                    Ihr
                          Ludwig Wittgenstein

27
XIII. St. Veitgasse, 17, bei Frau Sjögren   9.1.20
L. H. E.! Gestern erhielt ich von einem Herrn Viktor
Lautsch, der sich auf Herrn Lachs, Groag und Sie beruft

29.12.19

D. Mr. E., – I returned from Holland the day before yesterday. My meeting with Russell was most enjoyable. He wants to write an introduction to my book and I have agreed. Now I want to make another attempt to find a publisher. Surely, with an introduction by Russell the book will be a small risk for a publisher, as Russell is very well known. Perhaps you could write a letter to this effect to the gentleman who is to recommend me to Reclam[1]. If I cannot find a German publisher, Russell will have it printed in England. Since in that case he would have to take all sorts of steps, I beg you to let me know as soon as possible whether your efforts are likely to lead to any success at all. – – – I am in very low spirits these days. My relationship with my fellow men has strangely changed. What was all right when we met is now all wrong, and I am completely in despair. Incidentally, I foresee that it will take quite a long time before anything decisive happens. How glad I would be to see you again soon! Because the active use of my reason, which your presence makes possible, has some kind of soothing effect on me. – Give my respects and kind regards to your Mama.

Yours
Ludwig Wittgenstein

XIII. St. Veitgasse 17, c/o Frau Sjögren   9.1.20
D. Mr. E., – Yesterday I got a letter from one Mr. Viktor Lautsch[2], who gives Mr. Lachs, Groag, and you as references

[1] Despite the spelling (see German text), the publisher Ph. Reclam of Leipzig is presumably meant here and in later letters.
[2] 'Lautsch' may be a slip of the pen (occasioned by the 'Lachs' which follows) for 'Deutsch': there was a family of that name in Olmütz.

einen Brief, in welchem er mich um Unterstützung angeht. Da ich selbst kein Geld besitze und den Herrn nicht kenne, so schicke ich ihm vorderhand nur sehr wenig Geld und etwas Wäsche, die ich entbehren kann und bitte Sie vielmals, mir näheres über den Bittsteller zu schreiben. Vielleicht könnte sich meine Schwester Mining seiner annehmen. Je eher Sie mir antworten desto besser!

Da fällt mir ein, daß ich auch Ihr letztes liebes Schreiben noch nicht beantwortet habe. Ich lag aber mit Influenza zu Bett als es ankam. Auf die religieusen Bemerkungen gehe ich ein andermal ein. Sie scheinen mir noch nicht klar genug. Auch ich fühle jetzt klarer über die Sache als vor einem Monat. Alles das muß sich, glaube ich, viel richtiger sagen lassen. (Oder gar nicht, was noch wahrscheinlicher ist.)

Empfehlen Sie mich bitte herzlichst Ihrer verehrten Frau Mutter.

Ihr
Ludwig Wittgenstein

28

Lieber H. Engelmann! 26.1.20

Ihr liebes Schreiben hat mir sehr wohl getan. Es ist merkwürdig, daß ich wirklich in den letzten Tagen in einem mir schrecklichen Zustand war und auch jetzt ist die Sache noch nicht vorüber. Was mir so viele Qualen verursacht will ich Ihnen noch nicht sagen. Aber schon das Gefühl, daß jemand der den Menschen versteht, an mich denkt, ist gut. Die Geschichte vom Starez Sossima habe ich noch nicht gelesen und ich glaube eigentlich nicht, daß sie jetzt zu mir sprechen wird. – Nun wir werden ja sehen, was aus mir wird. – Ich habe gleich nach Empfang Ihres vorletzten Schreibens an Ficker um das Manuskript und an

and begs me to support him. Since I have no money myself and do not know the gentleman, I am sending him for the time being only very little money and some underwear I can spare, and I request you urgently to let me have more information about the petitioner. Perhaps my sister Mining could help him. The sooner you answer me, the better!

It just occurs to me that I myself have not yet answered your last kind letter. However, I was in bed with influenza when it arrived. I will deal another time with your remarks on religion. They are still not clear enough, it seems to me. I, too, feel that I am seeing the matter more clearly than a month ago. It must be possible, I believe, to say all these things much more adequately. (Or not at all, which is even more likely.)

Please give my respects and kind regards to your revered mother.

Yours
Ludwig Wittgenstein

28

Dear Mr. Engelmann,   26.1.20

Your kind letter has done me good. It is strange, I really was in the last few days in a state that was terrifying to myself, and the matter is not yet over. I don't want to tell you yet what it is that causes me so much torment. But simply to feel that someone who understands man[1] is thinking of me is soothing. I have not yet read the story of the *Starets* Zossima,[2] and I somehow do not think it will appeal to me at the moment. – Well, we shall see what will become of me. – After receiving your last letter but one I wrote immediately to Ficker[3] for the manu-

[1] Here Wittgenstein had first written 'life', then crossed it out and substituted 'man'.

[2] Dostoevsky's *Brothers Karamazov*, and the figure of the *Starets* in particular had long been favourite subjects of Wittgenstein's meditations and conversations with his intimate friends. See also p. 80 below.

[3] II. 3.

Russell um die Einleitung geschrieben. Noch habe ich aber nichts gekriegt.

Soll ich schon vorher an Reklam schreiben oder erst wenn ich ihm das Zeug schicke?

Möchte es Ihnen halbwegs gut gehen!

Viele Grüße.

Ihr dankbarer

Ludwig Wittgenstein

P.S. Soeben erhalte ich einen Brief von Ficker (aber noch kein Manuskript) worin er schreibt er müsse das Erscheinen des *Brenner* einstellen wenn er nicht sein ganzes Hab und Gut verlieren will. Kann man ihm helfen??

L.W.

29

19.2.20

L. H. E.! Ich habe wieder einmal das Bedürfnis Ihnen zu schreiben. Ich habe vor wenigen Tagen erfahren, daß ich die Einleitung Russells zu meiner Arbeit erst in einigen Wochen erwarten darf und habe dies auch Reklam mitgeteilt. Hoffentlich vergeht ihm bis dahin nicht die Lust. Meine äußeren Verhältnisse sind jetzt sehr traurig und wirken aufreibend auf mein Inneres. Dabei fehlt mir jeder Halt. Das einzig Gute, was ich jetzt habe, ist, daß ich den Kindern öfters in der Schule Märchen vorlese. Das gefällt ihnen und ist mir eine Erleichterung.

Aber sonst steht es mies mit Ihrem

Ludwig Wittgenstein

30

24.4.20

L. H. E.! Schon unerhört lange habe ich von Ihnen nichts mehr gehört! Schreiben Sie mir doch wieder eine Zeile. Mir ist es in der letzten Zeit sehr elend gegangen und auch jetzt fürchte ich noch, es möchte mich eines Tages der Teufel holen. Das ist kein Spaß!

28

script and to Russell for the introduction. So far, however, nothing has reached me.

Shall I write to Reclam in advance or only when I send off the stuff?

May things go passably well, with you!

Kind regards.

Yours gratefully
Ludwig Wittgenstein

P.S. I have just received a letter from Ficker (but no manuscript yet) in which he writes that he must stop publication of *Der Brenner* if he does not want to lose all he has. Can anything be done for him? ?

L.W.

29

19.2.20

D. Mr. E., – Once again I have the urge to write to you. I learnt only a few days ago that it will be several weeks before I can expect to get Russell's introduction, and I have informed Reclam accordingly. I hope he will not lose interest in the meantime. The external conditions of my life are very pitiable, and this is wearing down my morale. And I have nothing to hold on to. The one good thing in my life just now is that I sometimes read fairy-tales to the children at school. It pleases them and relieves the strain on me.

But otherwise things are in a mess for yours truly

Ludwig Wittgenstein

30

24.4.20

D. Mr. E., – I have not heard from you for an unconscionable time! Do drop me a line again. I have had a very miserable time lately, and I am still afraid the devil will come and take me one day. I am not joking!

Russells Einleitung zu meinem Buch ist jetzt hier und wird in's Deutsche übersetzt. Es ist ein Gebräu mit dem ich nicht einverstanden bin, aber da ich es nicht geschrieben habe, so macht mir das nicht viel.

Meine Adresse ist jetzt: III. Rasumofskygasse 24 (bei Herrn Zimmermann). Dieser Wohnungswechsel war von Operationen begleitet, an die ich nur zu denken brauche, damit es mir schwummerlich wird.

Schreiben Sie bald!

Ihr treuer
Ludwig Wittgenstein

Bitte empfehlen Sie mich wärmstens Ihrer verehrten lieben Frau Mutter, an die ich oft mit Dankbarkeit denke.

31

[8.5.20]

L. H. E.! Herzlichsten Dank für Ihre liebe Einladung. Zu Pfingsten kann ich zwar nicht kommen, aber nach meiner Prüfung werde ich es bestimmt tun. Zweig habe ich gesehen und manches mit ihm besprochen, wie er Ihnen wohl erzählen wird.

Mein Buch wird wahrscheinlich nicht gedruckt werden, da ich mich nicht entschließen konnte es mit Russells Einleitung, die in der Übersetzung noch viel unmöglicher aussieht als im Original, erscheinen zu lassen. – Sonst geht es mir ziemlich mies und ich hätte eine Aussprache mit Ihnen dringend nötig. Aber wir müssen eben noch etwas zuwarten.

Bitte empfehlen Sie mich wärmstens Ihrer verehrten Frau Mutter und sein Sie herzlichst gegrüßt von Ihrem
Ludwig Wittgenstein

Russell's introduction to my book has come and is being translated into German. He has brewed up a mixture with which I don't agree, but as I have not written it I don't mind much.

My new address is: III. Rasumofskygasse 24 (c/o Herr Zimmermann). This change of home was accompanied by operations which I can never remember without a sinking feeling.

Write soon!

Ever yours

Ludwig Wittgenstein

Please pass on my respects and kindest regards to your revered dear mother whom I often remember with gratitude.

31

[8.5.20]

D. Mr. E., – Sincere thanks for your kind invitation. I cannot come at Whitsun, but shall certainly do so after my exam. I have seen Zweig and discussed a number of things with him, as he presumably will tell you.

My book will probably not be printed, as I could not bring myself to have it published with Russell's introduction, which looks even more impossible in translation than it does in the original. – Apart from that I am in pretty poor shape and urgently need a talk with you. But we shall have to wait a little longer.

Please give my respects and best wishes to your revered mother. Kind regards to you from yours

Ludwig Wittgenstein

30.5.20

L. H. E.! Warum höre ich gar nichts mehr von Ihnen?!
(Wahrscheinlich, weil Sie mir nicht schreiben.) Ich möchte
mich wieder einmal ausleeren; es ist mir in der letzten
Zeit höchst miserabel gegangen. Natürlich nur durch
meine eigene Niedrigkeit und Gemeinheit. Ich habe
fortwährend daran gedacht, mir das Leben zu nehmen
und auch jetzt spukt dieser Gedanke noch in mir herum. *Ich
bin ganz und gar gesunken.* Möge es Ihnen nie so gehen! Ob
ich mich noch werde aufrichten können? Wir werden ja
sehen. – – – Reklam nimmt mein Buch nicht. Mir ist es
jetzt Wurst, und das ist gut.

Schreiben Sie *bald.*

Ihr
Ludwig Wittgenstein

33

[21.6.20]

L. H. E.! Vielen Dank für Ihren lieben Brief. Er hat mich
sehr gefreut und mir dadurch vielleicht ein wenig geholfen,
wenn auch nicht im Meritorischen meiner Angelegenheit,
denn da ist mir von außen nicht zu helfen. – Ich bin
nämlich in einem Zustand, in dem ich schon öfters im
Leben war, und der mir sehr furchtbar ist: Es ist der
Zustand *wenn man über eine bestimmte Tatsache nicht hinweg
kommt.* Daß dieser Zustand kläglich ist weiß ich. Aber es
gibt nur ein Mittel gegen ihn, das ich sehe, das ist eben
mit der Tatsache fertig werden. Da ist es aber genau
so, wie wenn jemand, der nicht schwimmen kann, in's
Wasser gefallen ist und nun mit Händen und Füßen
herumschlägt und fühlt, daß er sich nicht oben erhalten
kann. In dieser Lage bin ich jetzt. Ich weiß, daß der Selbstmord immer eine Schweinerei ist. Denn seine eigene
Vernichtung *kann* man gar nicht wollen und jeder, der

30.5.20

D. Mr. E., – Why don't I hear from you any more?![1]
(Presumably because you don't write to me.) I feel like
completely emptying myself again; I have had a most
miserable time lately. Of course only as a result of my own
baseness and rottenness. I have continually thought of
taking my own life, and the idea still haunts me sometimes.
I have sunk to the lowest point. May you never be in that
position! Shall I ever be able to raise myself up again?
Well, we shall see. – – – Reclam will not have my
book. I don't care any more, and that is a good thing.

Write *soon*.

Yours
Ludwig Wittgenstein

33

[21.6.20]

D. Mr. E., – Many thanks for your kind letter, which has
given me much pleasure and thereby perhaps helped me
a little, although as far as the merits of my case are concerned I am beyond any outside help. – In fact I am in
a state of mind that is terrible to me. I have been through
it several times before: it is the state of *not being able to get
over a particular fact.* It is a pitiable state, I know. But there
is only one remedy that I can see, and that is of course to
come to terms with that fact. But this is just like what
happens when a man who can't swim has fallen into the
water and flails about with his hands and feet and feels that
he *cannot* keep his head above water. That is the position I
am in now. I know that to kill oneself is always a dirty
thing to do. Surely one *cannot* will one's own destruction,
and anybody who has visualized what is in practice involved

[1] V. 6.

sich einmal den Vorgang beim Selbstmord vorgestellt hat, weiß, daß der Selbstmord immer eine *Überrumpelung* seiner selbst ist. Nichts aber ist ärger, als sich selbst überrumpeln zu müssen.

Alles läuft natürlich darauf hinaus, daß ich keinen Glauben habe!

Nun wir werden sehen! —

Bitte danken Sie in meinem Namen Ihrer verehrten Frau Mutter für ihren lieben Brief. Ich komme bestimmt nach Olmütz, weiß aber noch nicht wann. Hoffentlich geht es recht bald.

Ihr

Ludwig Wittgenstein

34

19.7.20

L. H. E.! Ich bin wortbrüchig geworden. Ich werde — wenigstens vorläufig — nicht zu Ihnen kommen. — Mein Plan für diese Ferien war ursprünglich, zuerst nach Olmütz und dann auf die Hochreit zu gehen. Je näher aber die Zeit herankam, umsomehr graute mir vor dieser Art, mir die Zeit zu vertreiben. (Denn selbst das Reden mit Ihnen — so genußreich es für mich ist — wäre mir jetzt in meiner zweifelhaften inneren Lage, nur ein Zeitvertreib). Ich sehnte mich nach irgend einer regelmäßigen Arbeit, welche — wenn ich mich nicht irre — für meinen gegenwärtigen Zustand noch das Erträglichste ist. Eine solche Arbeit scheine ich gefunden zu haben: Ich bin als Gärtnergehilfe im Stift Klosterneuburg für die Zeit meiner Ferien aufgenommen. (Wie es mir da gehen wird, wird sich zeigen). Ich fahre also jetzt weder nach Olmütz noch auf die Hochreit. Meine Adresse bleibt Rasumofskygasse etc. Ich werde Ihnen wieder schreiben. Bitte entschuldigen Sie mich bei Ihrer verehrten Frau Mutter.

Ihr

Ludwig Wittgenstein

in the act of suicide knows that suicide is always a *rushing of one's own defences*. But nothing is worse than to be forced to take oneself by surprise.

Of course it all boils down to the fact that I have no faith! *Well, we shall see! –*

Please thank your revered mother in my name for her kind letter. I will certainly come to Olmütz, but I don't know when. I do hope I can make it soon.

Yours
Ludwig Wittgenstein

34

19.7.20

D. Mr. E., – I have broken my word. I shall not come your way, at least for the time being. My plan for the holiday was to go first to Olmütz and then to the Hochreit. But the closer the time came, the more I felt aghast at this way of passing time. (For in my present dubious state of mind even talking to you – much as I enjoy it – would be no more than a pastime.) I was longing for some kind of regular work, which, of all the things I can do in my present condition, is the most nearly bearable, if I am not mistaken. It seems I have found such a job: I have been taken on as an assistant gardener at the Klosterneuburg Monastery for the duration of my holiday. (How life is going to treat me there, we shall see.) So I am not going either to Olmütz or on the Hochreit. My address remains Rasumofskygasse etc. I shall write again. Please give my apologies to your revered mother.

Yours
Ludwig Wittgenstein

[20.8.20]

L. H. E.! Schon *sehr* lange habe ich nichts von Ihnen gehört. Schreiben Sie mir doch eine Zeile: wie es Ihnen geht u.s.w.! Mein Aufenthalt in Klosterneuburg geht jetzt zu Ende; in 3 Tagen ziehe ich wieder nach Wien und warte auf Anstellung. Die Gartenarbeit war gewiß das Vernünftigste, was ich in den Ferien habe machen können. Wenn die Arbeit am Abend getan ist, so bin ich müde und fühle mich dann nicht unglücklich. Freilich graut mir etwas vor meinem künftigen Leben. Es müßte mit allen Teufeln zugehen, wenn es nicht sehr traurig ja unmöglich wird. – – – Ich weiß nicht in welcher Stimmung Sie sind, aber eine Aufheiterung kann man immer vertragen und darum schicke ich Ihnen hier einen Zeitungsausschnitt: so ziemlich das Unglaublichste was ich je gelesen habe. Heben Sie sich ihn, auf oder schicken Sie ihn mir zurück, aber zerreißen Sie ihn nicht! Ist es denkbar, daß Sie wieder einmal nach Wien kommen? Das wäre sehr schön. – Bitte empfehlen Sie mich Ihrer verehrten Frau Mutter *herzlichst* und schreiben Sie – aber wirklich! – bald Ihrem Sie bestens grüßenden

Ludwig Wittgenstein

P.S. Meine Schwester Mining ist besorgt, weil sie keine Antwort auf einen Brief erhalten hat, den sie Ihnen geschrieben hat. Sie ist aber nicht böse!

L.W.

Lieber Herr Engelmann!   11.10.20

Das merkwürdige Format dieses Briefes erklären Sie sich, bitte, so, daß ich zuerst jemand anderem habe schreiben wollen und diesen Anfang weggerissen habe. Warum ich

[20.8.20]

D. Mr. E., – Have been *very* long without news from you. Please drop me a line: how you are, etc.! My stay at Klosterneuburg is coming to an end; in three days I shall go back to Vienna and wait for a job. I am sure the gardening work was the most sensible thing I could have done in my holidays. In the evening when the work is done, I am tired, and then I do not feel unhappy. I have rather grim forebodings, though, about my future life. For unless all the devils in hell pull the other way, my life is bound to become very sad if not impossible. – – – I don't know what mood you are in, but we can always do with something to cheer us up, and so I enclose a newspaper cutting: quite unbelievable, beats almost anything else I have ever read.[1] Keep it or return it, but don't tear it up! Is it conceivable that you might be coming to Vienna again? That would be very fine. – Please pass on my respects and *very sincere* greetings to your revered mother, and do – but really do – write soon to yours ever

Ludwig Wittgenstein

P.S. My sister Mining is worried because she has had no reply to a letter she wrote to you. But she is not cross!

L.W.

Dear Mr. Engelmann, 11.10.20

The odd format of this letter[2] is explained by the fact that I first wanted to write to someone else, and then tore

---

[1] A promotional essay on 'A School of Wisdom' by Count Hermann Keyserling from the Vienna *Neue Freie Presse* of 6 August 1920.

[2] The top half of the first page of writing paper was torn off.

aber Striche gemacht und nicht gleich auf den vorge-
druckten Linien zu schreiben angefangen habe, können
Sie sich nicht erklären, und wenn Sie hundert Jahre
darüber nachdenken. Mit dieser Einleitung habe ich aber
bald die halbe Seite verschmiert und ich hätte sie also
auch einfach abreißen können.

Ich bin jetzt endlich Volksschullehrer und zwar in
einem sehr schönen und kleinen Nest, es heißt Trattenbach
(bei Kirchberg am Wechsel, N.Ö.). Die Arbeit in der
Schule macht mir Freude und ich brauche sie notwendig;
sonst sind bei mir gleich alle Teufel los. Wie gerne möchte
ich Sie sehen und sprechen! ! ! ! ! Vieles ist vorgefallen;
ich habe einige Operationen vorgenommen die *sehr*
schmerzhaft waren, aber gut abgelaufen sind. D.h. es fehlt
mir zwar jetzt hie und da ein Glied, aber besser ein paar
Glieder weniger und, die man hat, gesund. Gestern habe
ich im *Nathan dem Weisen* gelesen; ich finde ihn herrlich.
Mir scheint, Sie mögen ihn nicht? – Könnten Sie nicht
vielleicht zu Weihnachten nach Wien kommen?? Über-
legen Sie sich's! Schreiben Sie *bald* wie es Ihnen geht.
Empfehlen Sie mich *vielmals* Ihrer verehrten Frau Mutter,
an die ich immer wieder mit größter Dankbarkeit denke.

Herzliche Grüße
Ihr
Ludwig Wittgenstein

37

31.10.20

L. H. E.! Bitte tun Sie mir folgenden großen Gefallen!:
Sein Sie so gut, die beiden Bände Frege, *Grundgesetze der
Arithmetik*, REKOMMANDIERT & EXPRESS an die folgende
Adresse zu schicken: Fräulein Anna Knaur p. A. Faber,
Heinrichsthal bei Lettowitz, Mähren. Diese Dame wird
nicht etwa Logik studieren, sondern mir das Buch ungelesen
mitbringen. Da sie schon am 10. abfährt, so hat die
Geschichte große Eile. Wenn Sie zu Weihnachten kommen,

off that beginning. But why I drew my own lines instead of writing straightaway on the printed ones you'll never fathom though you might think about it for a hundred years. Well, in scribbling this introduction I have nearly used up the half page, so I could have simply torn it off.

At last I have become a primary-school teacher, and I am working in a beautiful and tiny place called Trattenbach (near Kirchberg-am-Wechsel, Lower Austria). I am happy in my work at school, and I do need it badly, or else all the devils in Hell break loose inside me. How much I should like to see you and talk to you! ! ! ! ! A great deal has happened. I have carried out several operations which were *very* painful but went off well. I.e. I may miss a limb from time to time – but better have a few limbs less and the remaining ones sound. Yesterday I looked at a passage in *Nathan der Weise*:[1] I find it superb. I seem to remember you don't like the play? Couldn't you possibly come to Vienna for Christmas?? Think it over! Write *soon* and tell me how you are. Give my respects and *all* good wishes to your revered mother, whom I remember so often with deep gratitude.

> Kindest regards from
> Yours
> Ludwig Wittgenstein

37

31.10.20

D. Mr. E., – Would you do me the following great favour! Will you kindly send the two volumes of Frege, *Grundgesetze der Arithmetik* REGISTERED & EXPRESS to the following address: Miss Anna Knaur, c/o Faber, Heinrichsthal, near Lettowitz, Moravia. This lady will not herself study logic, but will bring me the book unread. As she will leave on the 10th, the matter is very pressing. When you come

[1] The play by Lessing.

kriegen Sie den Frege wieder. Vorläufig vielen Dank!
Ich freue mich schon sehr mit Ihnen zu reden; ich habe
ein große Bedürfnis danach.

Ihr

L. Wittgenstein

38

Lieber H. E.!   2.1.21

Vielen Dank für Ihren Brief. Es hat mir leid getan,
daß ich Sie zu Weihnachten nicht gesehen habe. Daß Sie
sich vor *mir* verstecken wollen, hat mich etwas komisch
berührt und zwar aus folgendem Grunde: Ich bin seit
mehr als einem Jahr moralisch vollkommen tot! Daraus
können Sie nun auch beurteilen, ob es mir gut geht. Ich
bin einer von den Fällen, die vielleicht heute nicht so selten
sind: Ich hatte eine Aufgabe, habe sie nicht gemacht und
gehe jetzt daran zu Grunde. Ich hätte mein Leben zum
Guten wenden sollen und ein Stern werden. Ich bin aber
auf der Erde sitzen geblieben und nun gehe ich nach und
nach ein. Mein Leben ist eigentlich sinnlos geworden und
darum besteht es nur mehr aus überflüssigen Episoden.
Meine Umgebung merkt das freilich nicht und verstünde
es auch nicht; aber ich weiß, daß es mir am Grundlegenden
fehlt.

Sein Sie froh, wenn Sie nicht verstehen, was ich da
schreibe. – – –

Auf Wiedersehen

Ihr

Ludw Wittgenstein

39

L. H. E.!   7.2.21

Ich bin jetzt nicht im Stande meinen Zustand brieflich
zu analysieren. Ich glaube – nebenbei – nicht, daß Sie ihn
ganz verstehen. Zu allem ist mein körperliches Befinden

40

for Christmas, you shall get the Frege back. In the meantime many thanks! I am greatly looking forward to talking with you; I feel an urgent need for it.

Yours
L. Wittgenstein

38

Dear Mr. E., 2.1.21

Many thanks for your letter. I was sorry not to have seen you at Christmas. It struck me as rather funny that you should want to hide from *me*, for the following reason: I have been morally dead for more than a year! From that you can judge for yourself whether I am fine or not. I am one of those cases which perhaps are not all that rare today: I had a task, did not do it, and now the failure is wrecking my life. I ought to have done something positive with my life, to have become a star in the sky. Instead of which I remained stuck on earth, and now I am gradually fading out. My life has really become meaningless and so it consists only of futile episodes. The people around me do not notice this and would not understand; but I know that I have a fundamental deficiency. Be glad of it, if you don't understand what I am writing here. — — —

Auf Wiedersehen
Yours
Ludw Wittgenstein

39

D. Mr. E., 7.2.21

I cannot at present analyse my state in a letter. I don't think – by the way – that you quite understand it. On top of everything else I am in fairly poor condition physically

4I

jetzt ziemlich schlecht und keine Hoffnung auf baldige Besserung. Ihr Kommen wäre mir in der nächsten Zeit nicht eigentlich erwünscht. Ich fürchte, wir könnten jetzt nichts Rechtes mit einander anfangen. Verschieben wir's bis zu den großen Ferien. (Wenn *Sie* dann Lust haben.) Vielleicht leben wir dann schon nicht mehr.

Ihr

Wittgenstein

40

L. H. E.! [25.4.21]

Heute nur wenige Zeilen, weil ich körperlich nicht gut beisammen bin. Es wäre vielleicht gut wenn wir uns wieder träfen, aber lieber nicht zu Beginn der großen Ferien, sondern am Ende, also etwa Anfangs September. Es geht mir jetzt nicht so schlecht – innerlich – als damals als ich Ihnen zuletzt schrieb, wenn auch nicht wirklich gut; ja im Wesentlichen schlecht. Mehr kann ich jetzt nicht schreiben. Auf Wiedersehen im September! Bis dahin möge uns Gott helfen!

Ihr

L Wittgenstein

41

5.8.21 Skjolden i Sogn   Norwegen

L. H. E.! bei Herrn Drægni

Nun bin ich wieder in Skjolden, wo ich schon vor dem Krieg ein Jahr lang war. Das Buch, das Sie mir versprachen, habe ich nicht mehr bekommen (Hätten Sie mir wenigstens geschrieben, was es war). In den ersten Tagen des September komme ich zurück und bleibe bis zum Schulanfang in Wien. Werden Sie zu dieser Zeit auch nach Wien kommen? *Das wäre sehr schön!* Es hat sich sicher viel Gesprächsstoff angehäuft. Da fällt mir ein: Immer wieder schickt Ficker mir

42

and without hope of an early improvement. As a matter of fact, a visit from you would not suit me in the near future. Just now we would hardly know what to do with one another. Let's postpone it to the summer holidays. (If *you* feel like it then.)

Perhaps we shall no longer be alive by then.

Yours

Wittgenstein

40

D. Mr. E., [25.4.21]

Only a few lines today, as I am physically in poor shape. Perhaps it would be good for us to meet again, though not at the beginning of the summer holidays but at the end, say the beginning of September. My condition – I mean my state of mind – is not as bad as it was when I wrote you last; though it is not really good; in fact, basically it is bad. I can write no more now. Auf Wiedersehen next September! Until then may God help us!

Yours

L Wittgenstein

41

5.8.21 Skjolden i Sogn, Norway

D. Mr. E., c/o Mr. Drægni

I am again at Skjolden where I spent a year before the war. The book you promised me did not come in time. (If at least you had let me know what it was). I shall be back in the first days of September and will stay in Vienna until the beginning of term. Will you also be coming to Vienna at that time? *That would be splendid!* Surely topics of conversation have accumulated. That reminds me: Ficker keeps on sending me *Der Brenner*,

den *Brenner* zu und immer wieder nehme ich mir vor, ihm zu schreiben, er soll es bleiben lassen, weil ich den *Brenner* für einen Unsinn halte (eine christliche Zeitschrift ist eine Schmockerei) — aber ich komme doch nie dazu die Absage an Ficker zu schreiben weil ich zu einer längeren Erklärung nicht die Ruhe finde. Daraus sehen Sie übrigens, wie es mir geht.

Auf Wiedersehen
Ihr
Ludwig Wittgenstein

Arvid Sjögren der mit mir hier ist läßt Sie grüßen.

42

L. H. E.!   9.9.21
   Ihre Karte die ich gestern erhielt, hat mich etwas geärgert. Wir können uns *natürlich nicht mehr* sehen, da ich schon am 13ten nach Trattenbach fahre. Sie hätten doch wissen müssen, daß Sie wegen einer Wohnung in Wien nicht Verhandlungen mit Bekannten führen brauchten, sondern bei meiner Mutter *jederzeit* hätten wohnen können! Und daß nicht viel Zeit zu verlieren war, da meine Schule Mitte September beginnt, hätten Sie sich auch sagen können. Nun, wenn zu Weihnachten nicht wieder irgend welche überflüssige Dummheiten dazwischen kommen, so können wir uns vielleicht dann doch einmal sehen. Es tut mir leid, daß es nicht jetzt gegangen ist.

Ihr
L. Wittgenstein

43

L. H. E.!   23.10.21
   Ich möchte Ihnen gerne ein paar Worte schreiben, weil

44

and I keep on wanting to write to him to stop it, as I believe *Der Brenner* is nonsense (a Christian journal is intellectual make-believe) – but I never get down to sending the notice of cancellation to Ficker, as I cannot find sufficient peace and quiet to write a lengthy explanation. From this, incidentally, you can see how I am.

Auf Wiedersehen
Yours
Ludwig Wittgenstein

Arvid Sjögren, who is here with me, wants to be remembered to you.

42

D. Mr. E.,   9.9.21
Your card, which I received yesterday, has annoyed me a bit. *Of course we can no longer meet*, as I am going to Trattenbach on the 13th. Surely you must have known that there was no need to conduct negotiations with acquaintances about lodgings in Vienna when you could have stayed *any time* with my mother! You might also have considered that there was not much time to lose as my term starts in the middle of September. Well, provided we are not foiled again by avoidable stupidities, perhaps we'll be able to meet after all at Christmas. I am sorry it has not worked out now.

Yours
L. Wittgenstein

43

D. Mr. E.,   23.10.21
I should like to write you a few words as I have now

ich den *König der dunklen Kammer* jetzt gelesen habe. Das Stück hat auf mich keinen wirklich tiefen Eindruck gemacht, obwohl die große Weisheit darin offensichtlich ist – oder vielleicht gerade deshalb. Es hat mich nicht erschüttert (vielleicht ist das aber doch meine Schuld.) Es kommt mir so vor, als käme alle diese Weisheit schon aus dem Eiskasten; ich würde mich nicht sehr darüber wundern, zu hören, daß er das alles zusammengelesen und gehört, (wie ja so viele bei uns die christliche Weisheit) aber nicht eigentlich selber *gefühlt* hat. Vielleicht aber verstehe ich seinen Ton nicht; aber mir scheint er nicht der Ton eines von der Wahrheit *ergriffenen* Menschen zu sein. (*Wie etwa der Ton Ibsens.*) Es ist aber auch möglich, daß hier die Übersetzung für mich eine Kluft läßt, die ich nicht überbrücken kann. Ich habe immer *mit Interesse* gelesen, aber ohne gepackt zu werden. Das scheint mir kein gutes Zeichen zu sein. Denn der Stoff war danach um mich zu packen. Oder bin ich schon so stumpf, daß mich nichts mehr angreift? – auch möglich. – Auch habe ich keinen Augenblick die Empfindung, daß hier ein Drama vor sich geht, sondern ich verstehe nur abstrakt die Allegorie. Schreiben Sie mir doch auch Ihre Gedanken. Sie werden ein wenig gescheiter ausfallen, als wie die meinen. Kein Wunder! – Hier ist alles beim Alten. Ich bin so dumm und so unanständig wie immer. Nichts rührt sich in mir, was auf eine bessere Zukunft hindeuten würde. Vielleicht müßte ich durch einen äußeren Hieb erst ganz zerschlagen werden, damit wieder Leben in diesen Leichnam kommt. Sein Sie bestens gegrüßt. Empfehlen Sie mich vielmals Ihrer lieben Frau Mama.

Ihr
Ludw Wittgenstein

read *The King of the Dark Chamber*.[1] The play has not really made a deep impression on me, although the great wisdom in it is manifest – or possibly just because of that. I was not moved (but that may be my own fault). It seems to me as if all that wisdom has come out of the ice box; I should not be surprised to learn that he got it all second-hand by reading and listening (exactly as so many among us acquire their knowledge of Christian wisdom) rather than from his own genuine *feeling*. Perhaps I don't understand his tone; to me it does not ring like the tone of a man possessed by the truth. (*Like for instance Ibsen's tone*.) It is possible, however, that here the translation leaves a chasm which I cannot bridge. I read *with interest* throughout, but without being gripped. That does not seem to be a good sign. For this is a subject that could have gripped me – or have I become so deadened that nothing will touch me any longer? A possibility, no doubt. – Again, I do not feel for a single moment that here a drama is taking place, I merely understand the allegory in an abstract way. Let me know what you think. It will be a bit more intelligent than my effort. And no wonder! – Here everything is as it was. I am as stupid and rotten as ever. Nothing stirs in me that could be taken to indicate a better future. Perhaps I should first have to be shattered completely by a blow from outside, before new life could enter this corpse. Greetings to you and my respects and kind regards to your dear Mama.

Yours

Ludw Wittgenstein

[1] By Rabindranath Tagore. Wittgenstein evidently came to think better of this play. He gave a copy to his sister, Mrs. Stonborough, and L. Hänsel lists it as one of his favourite books (*Begegnungen und Auseinandersetzungen*, p. 321). In 1927 and 1928 at meetings with Schlick and one or two others Wittgenstein often would not discuss philosophical topics but preferred to read out poetry, particularly the poetry of Tagore.

44

[Postkarte]   [Poststempel 5.8.(22)]

L. H. E.! Sie hatten wahrhaftig keinen Grund zum
schlechten Gewissen und ich habe natürlich auch nie
daran gedacht. Die Arbeit ist bereits einmal gedruckt und
zwar in den *Annalen der Naturphilosophie* von Ostwald
(Heft 14). Diesen Druck betrachte ich aber als Raubdruck,
er ist voller Fehlern![1] In den nächsten Wochen aber erscheint
die Geschichte in London und zwar deutsch und englisch.
Wenn möglich werde ich Ihnen ein Exemplar schicken wenn
es Ihnen Spaß macht. Es würde mich sehr freuen, Sie im
Sommer wiederzusehen und vieles zu besprechen. Die Zeit
die Sie angeben ist mir sehr recht.

>   Ihr
>   L. Wittgenstein

45

L. H. E.!   10.8.22

Ich möchte Sie nur daran erinnern, daß wir ausgemacht
haben, Sie würden mich im August in Wien besuchen.
Vor einigen Tagen habe ich Ihnen ein Telegramm geschickt,
um Sie zu bitten, Sie möchten nicht vor dem 12. kommen,
weil ich bis dahin nicht in Wien sein kann, da ich in
Innsbruck eine Zusammenkunft mit meinem Bekannten
Russell aus England habe, der eigens meinetwegen nach
Innsbruck kommt, – so daß ich diese Sache nicht verschieben konnte.

Jetzt aber, d. h. von morgen an – denn heute bin ich
noch in Innsbruck – bleibe ich in Wien und stehe zu
Ihrer Verfügung; hoffentlich machen Sie davon Gebrauch.
Hier habe ich auch Ficker besucht der – um mich eines
seiner Lieblingswörter zu bedienen – ein sehr fragwürdiger
Mensch ist. D.h., ich weiß wirklich nicht, wie viel an ihm
echt und wieviel Charlatan ist. Aber, was geht das mich

---

[1] Sic.

[Postcard]   [Postmark 5.8.(22)]
D. Mr. E., – Surely there is not the slightest reason for
you to have a bad conscience; and, of course, I never
thought of it that way at all. The treatise has already been
printed once – in Ostwald's *Annalen der Naturphilosophie* (No.
14). However, I consider this a pirated edition: it is full of
errors. But in a few weeks the thing will come out in
London, in both German and English. If possible, I shall
send you a copy if it would amuse you. I should be very
glad to meet you this summer and discuss a lot of things.
The time you mention suits me perfectly.

Yours
L. Wittgenstein

D. Mr. E.,   10.8.22
I only want to remind you of our arrangement that you
should visit me in Vienna in August. A few days ago I
sent you a telegram to request you not to come before the
12th, because I cannot be in Vienna before then, as I have
an appointment in Innsbruck with my English acquaintance, Russell, who is coming to Innsbruck specially on
my account, – so I could not postpone that matter.

But now, i.e. from tomorrow – for I am still in Innsbruck
today – I shall be staying in Vienna and will be at your
disposal; I do hope you will make use of this opportunity.
Here one of my visits was to Ficker who – to use a favourite
term of his – is a most dubious person. I.e. I really don't
know how far he is genuine and how far a charlatan. Still,
what business is it of mine! So I hope very much to see

an! Also ich hoffe sehr, Sie im August zu sehen. Zu meiner
großen Schande muß ich gestehen, daß die Zahl der
Menschen mit denen ich reden kann sich immer mehr
verringert. Mit Ihnen aber, glaube ich, hätte ich noch
viel zu reden.

Ihr
Ludw Wittgenstein

46

[Postkarte]   [Poststempel 17.8.22]

 Vielen Dank für Ihre Karte. Es ist mir sehr recht, wenn
Sie zwischen dem 20ten und 25ten nach Wien kommen.
Aber *tun* Sie's nur auch wirklich!!

Auf Wiedersehn
Ihr
L. Wittgenstein

47

[Postkarte]

L. H. E.!   [Poststempel 24.8.22]

 Wenn Sie nach Wien kommen, wie ich noch immer hoffe,
obwohl Sie es versprochen haben, so bitte kommen Sie
vor dem 1./9., da ich dann auf die Hochreit fahre. Und
oben könnte ich nichts von Ihnen haben. Sonst aber
zwischen dem 8./9. und 13./9.; während dieser Tage werde
ich wieder in Wien sein. Es ist schade daß man sich so
wenig auf Sie verlassen kann, daß man trotz 100 Vera-
bredungen immer gänzlich im Ungewissen ist.

Ihr
L. Wittgenstein

48

Lieber Herr Engelmann!   14.9.22

 Verzeihen Sie, daß ich Ihnen erst heute das Geld schicke.

50

you in August. To my great shame I must confess that the number of people to whom I can talk is constantly diminishing. But with you, I believe, I should still have a lot to talk about.

Yours
Ludw Wittgenstein

46

[Postcard]   [Postmark 17.8.22]
   Many thanks for your card. It will suit me very well if you come to Vienna between the 20th and the 25th. Now stick to it and do come *really*! !

Auf Wiedersehen
Yours
L. Wittgenstein

47

[Postcard]
D. Mr. E.,   [Postmark 24.8.22]
   If you are coming to Vienna, as I am still hoping although you have promised it, please come before 1.9, as I am leaving for the Hochreit then. And up there I should not benefit at all from your visit. Otherwise between 8.9 and 13.9 when I shall again be in Vienna. It is a pity that one can rely on you so little that in spite of a hundred arrangements everything is as uncertain as ever.

Yours
L. Wittgenstein

48

Dear Mr. Engelmann,   14.9.22
   Forgive me for sending you the money only today. It

5I

Es ist pure Schlamperei, daß Sie es noch nicht bekommen haben.

Ihr Aufenthalt in Wien war sehr angenehm für mich. Was wir damals von einer eventuellen Flucht nach Rußland sprachen, das spukt noch immer in meinem Kopf herum; besonders nämlich darum weil ich vor ein paar Tagen in dem zukünftigen Ort meiner Lehrtätigkeit (Hassbach bei Neunkirchen, N.Ö.) war und dort von meiner neuen Umgebung (Lehrer, Pfarrer etc.) einen *sehr* unangenehmen Eindruck bekommen habe. Gott weiß, wie das werden wird! ? ! Es sind *gar* keine Menschen, nur ekelhafte Larven. Schreiben Sie mir bald dorthin, Ihre Gedanken, etc..

Seien Sie gegrüßt von

Ihrem alten
Ludw Wittgenstein

49

L. H. E.!   [Ohne Datum, aber nach 15.11.24]

Hier schicke ich Ihnen die Zeitungsausschnitte, von denen ich Ihnen schon einmal erzählt habe. Ich habe sie wieder aufgefunden und war beim Lesen von neuem überrascht. Es geht mir jetzt aus verschiedenen äußeren Gründen – vielleicht auch aus inneren Gründen – besser als im Sommer. Heben Sie die Ausschnitte auf!

Ihr
L. Wittgenstein

50

L. H. E.!   24.2.25

Vielen Dank für Ihren Brief. Ich habe manchmal an Sie gedacht, konnte mich aber nicht entschließen, Ihnen zu schreiben, da mir die Verbindung zwischen uns auf

was sheer negligence on my part that you did not get it before.

Your stay in Vienna was very pleasant for me. The idea of a possible flight to Russia which we talked about keeps on haunting me. The main reason for this is that I visited a few days ago the place where I am going to teach (Hassbach, near Neunkirchen, Lower Austria), and had a very disagreeable impression of the new environment there (teachers, parish priest, etc.) God knows how this is going to work out! ? ![1] They are not human *at all* but loathsome worms. Do write to me there soon and tell me what you are thinking, etc.

Kind regards from

Yours ever
Ludw Wittgenstein

49

D. Mr. E.,   [Undated, but later than 15.11.24]

I am sending you the newspaper cuttings I mentioned to you once before.[2] I found them again and was again surprised when I read them. For various external reasons – possibly also for internal reasons – I am now in better shape than last summer. Keep the cuttings together!

Yours
L. Wittgenstein

50

D. Mr. E.,   24.2.25

Many thanks for your letter. I have thought of you at times but could not make up my mind to write to you, as

[1] In the event Wittgenstein spent only a short time at Hassbach, moving almost immediately to Puchberg.

[2] Prize-winning poems by workers: 'Ein ehernes Lied' by Hans Winterl ('Grauer Geselle, ich weih' dich dem Frieden,/Trotziger Stahl wir wollen dich schmieden,/. . .'), 'Die Magd' by Symphorosa Iglhaut, etc.

irgend eine Weise unterbrochen schien. Gewiß, Sie sind nicht anständig, aber Sie sind doch noch *viel, viel* anständiger als ich. Von mir will ich nicht reden. –

Wohl fühle ich mich nicht: aber nicht weil mir meine Schweinerei zu schaffen machte, sondern innerhalb der Schweinerei. Ich leide sehr unter den Menschen, oder Unmenschen, mit welchen ich lebe. Kurz alles wie immer! Daß Sie nach Palästina gehen wollen ist das, was mir Ihren Brief erfreulich und hoffnungsvoll macht. Das ist vielleicht richtig und kann eine seelische Wirkung haben. Vielleicht wollte ich mich Ihnen anschließen. Würden Sie mich mitnehmen? Jedenfalls möchte ich ein langes Gespräch mit Ihnen haben. Ich muß über vieles sprechen, was mir *wichtig* ist und halte das *Reden* darüber selbst für *wichtig* und nicht für Geschwätz. Sie würden mir also einen Gefallen tun, wenn Sie, womöglich zu Ostern, nach Wien kämen. Über ernste Dinge ausführlich zu schreiben wäre natürlich Zeitvergeudung.

Seien Sie gegrüßt von Ihrem
Ludw Wittgenstein

Meine Adresse ist jetzt: Otterthal
Post Kirchberg am Wechsel, Nieder-Österr.

51

L. H. E.   [Poststempel Lewes (England) 19.8.25]

Ich habe Ihnen nichts zu verzeihen. Was Sie mir gesagt haben, war zum größten Teil wahr (wenn auch vielleicht manches überflüßig war) und nur in unserem letzten Gespräch haben Sie mich nicht verstanden. Aber wie könnte ich verlangen, daß Sie mich verstehen, wenn ich mich selbst kaum verstehe! Es war gut, daß ich Sie getroffen habe: es hat mir einige gute Stunden verschafft. Ich bin jetzt in England bei Keynes aber noch ebenso unklar wie sonst. Ob ich Sie in Olmütz werde besuchen können, weiß ich nicht sicher. Ich werde noch darüber schreiben. Sie wissen wieviel mir unser Beisammensein gibt. Ich weiß daß

the contact between us seemed somehow broken. It is true that you are not decent, still you are *vastly more* decent than I. I don't want to speak about myself. –

Anyway I am not happy, and not because my rottenness troubles me, but within my rottenness. I suffer much from the human, or rather inhuman, beings with whom I live – in short it is all as usual! That you want to go to Palestine is the one piece of news that makes your letter cheering and hopeful for me. This may be the right thing to do and may have a spiritual effect. I might want to join you. Would you take me with you? In any case I should like to have a long talk with you. I must speak about many matters which are *important* to me, and I consider that to *talk* about them is also *important* and not just gassing. So you would do me a favour by coming to Vienna, if possible at Easter. To write long letters about serious matters would of course be a waste of time.

Kind regards from yours
Ludw Wittgenstein

My present address is: Otterthal,
near Kirchberg am Wechsel, Lower Austria

51

D. Mr. E.,   [Postmark Lewes, 19.8.25]

I have nothing to forgive you. What you told me was mostly true (though some of it perhaps superfluous), and it was only in our last talk that you did not understand me. But how could I expect you to understand me when I barely understand myself! It was good to have met you. It gave me a few good hours. I am in England, staying with Keynes, but as far away from clarity as ever. I am not sure whether I shall be able to visit you in Olmütz. I will let you know. You do know how much I gain from our meetings. I know that brilliance – the riches of the

55

Geistreichtum nicht das Gute ist und doch wollte ich
jetzt, ich könnte in einem geistreichen Augenblick sterben.

Ihr

L Wittgenstein

52

[Ansichtskarte mit der Schule in Ottertal]

L. H. E.! [Poststempel 9.9.25]

Besten Dank für beide Briefe, die ich heute *hier* erhielt.
Sie sehen daraus daß ich es noch einmal versuche. Es war
mir unmöglich noch nach Olmütz zu kommen, so gerne ich
es getan hätte. Praktischen Wert hätte es übrigens bestimmt
keinen gehabt. Im Notfalle werde ich wahrscheinlich nach
England gehen. Ich kann jetzt nicht mehr schreiben, weil
ich in den wichtigsten Dingen noch unentschlossen bin.

Ihr Wittgenstein

53

L. H. E.! [Ohne Datum]

Ich werde mich freuen Sie zu Weihnachten in Wien zu
sehen. Der Bau eines Wohnhauses würde mich auch sehr
interessieren. Ich bleibe vom 24./12. bis zum 2./1. in Wien.

Ihr L. Wittgenstein

Ich hätte auch allerlei Persönliches zu besprechen. Ob
wir uns diesmal verständigen können, wird sich ja zeigen.

spirit – is not the ultimate good, and yet I wish now I could die in a moment[1] of brilliance.

Yours

L Wittgenstein

52

[Picture postcard showing the school at Otterthal]

D. Mr. E.,   [Postmark 9.9.25]

Many thanks for both letters which reached me *here* today. You will see from this that I am trying once again. I could not manage to get to Olmütz, much as I should have liked to. Incidentally, it would certainly not have been of any practical use. In case of need I shall probably go to England. I cannot write any more now, because I am still undecided in the most important matters.

Yours Wittgenstein

53

D. Mr. E.,   [Undated]

I shall be glad to see you at Christmas in Vienna. I should also be very interested in the building of a house. I shall be in Vienna from 24.12 to 2.1.[2]

Yours L. Wittgenstein

I also have various personal matters to discuss with you. Whether we shall be able to understand each other this time will become clear soon enough.

---

[1] Here Wittgenstein had first written 'geistreichen Gespräch' ('brilliant conversation') then crossed out 'Gespräch' and substituted 'Augenblick' ('moment').

[2] Wittgenstein began working on the Kundmanngasse house in autumn 1926 (G. H. von Wright, *Biographical Sketch*, p. 11). This letter must have been written towards the end of 1925.

54

Lieber Herr Engelmann!   21.6.37

Danke für Ihren gütigen Brief. Mein fundamentaler
Eindruck von Ihrer Person kann sich durch das, was Sie
sagen nicht ändern und keine Einsicht in Ihr Wesen
könnte bewirken, daß es mich gereut Ihnen das Geständnis
geschickt zu haben. Ich wollte, wie ich vor kurzem in
Wien war, Ihrem Bruder die Sache mündlich erzählen
(d.i. den Inhalt jenes Schreibens) bin aber nicht dazugekommen. Aus irgend einem Grund fühle ich ein Widerstreben,
ihm den Brief schicken zu lassen, obwohl sein Inhalt für ihn
natürlich kein Geheimnis sein soll. Ich habe ihn (Ihren
Bruder) gesehen und ihm von dem Brief erzählt und gesagt
ich würde ihn wieder besuchen und ihm den Inhalt des
Briefes mitteilen, habe es aber dann hinausgeschoben und
bin nicht mehr dazugekommen. Vielleicht war es ein
Freudisches Hinausschieben. Ich bin jetzt auf kurze Zeit
in England; fahre vielleicht nach Rußland. Gott weiß, was
aus mir werden wird. Ich denke mit guten Gefühlen an
Sie. Möge es Ihnen irgendwie gut gehen!!! Danke für
alles was Sie in Ihrem Brief geschrieben haben!

Ihr
Ludwig Wittgenstein

Ich schicke dies nach Wien, damit es weiter befördert wird.

Trinity College
Cambridge
Dear Mr. Engelmann,   21.6.37

Thank you for your very kind letter. My fundamental impression of your person cannot be changed by what you say, and no insight into your character could make me regret having sent you the confession. When I was in Vienna recently, I wanted to tell your brother personally about the matter (i.e. the substance of that letter), but did not manage to. For some reason or other I am reluctant to have the letter sent to him although, of course, its substance is not meant to be kept secret from him. I did see him and told him about the existence of the letter, and said I would call again to inform him about the contents of the letter, but then I put it off and never got round to it. Perhaps this was a Freudian procrastination. I am now in England for a short stay; perhaps I shall go to Russia. God knows what will become of me. I think of you with friendly feelings. May things go well with you somehow or other ! ! ! Thank you for everything you wrote in your letter!

Yours
Ludwig Wittgenstein

I am sending this to Vienna for forwarding.

II. *Wittgenstein in Olmütz*

I

A description of the environment in which Wittgenstein spent several months in 1916 seems important to me, though not because Wittgenstein himself cared particularly where, or in what surroundings, he lived. It was different, of course, during his earlier and decisive period of work in Norway; but later in life – as I know – he was largely indifferent to his environment and accepted the most primitive material conditions and the lowliest social milieu. He was, on the other hand, excessively sensitive to, and dependent on, the disposition of the people whom he happened to encounter. So I hope that the following sketchy observations about the town in which he then lived and about its peculiarities will help the reader to visualize the slightly odd environment which Wittgenstein met in my parents' home and the circle of my close acquaintances, where he not only found life endurable but, in his particular frame of mind at the time, actually felt at ease.

My native city, Olmütz in Moravia, was a town with a cultural past still recognizable in its buildings. Olmütz was different from other towns in the region. It was in my time still an entrancing ruin of bygone days rising out of the spiritual lowlands of the twentieth century. A childhood spent between the flaking town houses grouped round two vast market-places, or in one of the crooked little lanes tightly crammed into the inadequate space of a former fortress, in houses with dark vaulted stairways, in flats consisting of a few huge and gloomy rooms with badly dilapidated floors of varnished boards, inhabited by the last offshoots of old and slowly dying burgher families – such a childhood will endow a man with a musical ear, as it were, for things past which must elude those brought up in more ordinary surroundings.

To explain the conditions in my parental home – which also were somewhat out of the ordinary – I have to mention that my father was a businessman who after a disastrous failure many years back had made a new start and built up a modest but reasonably comfortable livelihood for himself and his family as a representative of insurance companies. By comparison with former times, of course, the family lived in much reduced circumstances, and – far more important – my father, and doubly so my mother, felt for the rest of their lives *déclassé* in their social environment. The intensity of their feeling was quite out of proportion to the real situation. My mother in particular suffered deeply. The daughter of a doctor, long dead by then, who had been highly esteemed for his human and intellectual qualities, she could never get over the fact that our small-town society was dominated by families whom she considered upstarts. Indeed, within that social group a man's worth was gauged entirely in terms of money, wealth, and success in business. Thanks to my mother's personality and her warm-hearted ways, guests felt uncommonly at ease in our home; it pained her deeply that she could not treat them as generously as she would have liked to, and in truth her hospitality went often, if not always, beyond our means.

My parents were persons of cultivated taste. Though lacking in academic education, they were quite outstanding in their milieu for their literary judgement, which was good because based on human understanding. (My father, for instance, working as a young commercial apprentice in the home of a rich relative – though his ambition was to become an actor – was an enthusiastic reader of Gottfried Keller, who at that time, in the seventies and eighties of the last century, was still a fairly obscure author nowhere appreciated at his true worth.)

All the more did my parents shun the upstart small-town society which in turn, with the bland complacency customary in such cases, looked down on what appeared to them a poverty-stricken, yet presumptuous isolation.

The few friends whom I had among the young people of my generation and who came to our house revered my mother, who participated in our evening gatherings with much sympathy, though mainly in the role of a listener. It was felt by all that the exceptional warmth and homeliness of those evenings were due to her, and Wittgenstein in particular – lonely, forlorn, marooned in the desert, as he tended to feel anywhere outside his family circle in Vienna – was moved to rapturous feelings of gratitude. Our friends, in good-humoured irony, called our home – openly, of course, not behind our backs – the '*Palais* on the Mauritz-platz'. The Mauritzplatz was in the city centre, but our flat was in a back wing, and our windows looked out on the glorious ancient church of St. Maurice. None of the prominent families, however, lived in that district.

What seemed at first sight striking in Wittgenstein's choice of the company he kept in Olmütz, was, of course, his position as a young man from a prominent Viennese millionaire's family. Inconspicuous as the whole episode was, such details invariably get around in a small town. People could not square this with their customary ideas and remained baffled.

3

I will now describe my first encounter with Wittgenstein.

One afternoon the maid told me a gentleman wanted to see me. I went into the back room, a so-called 'Berlin chamber' which formed one corner of the flat and was lit only through a narrow window giving out on the courtyard. This was the room where we sat with our friends in the evenings. As I entered, the afternoon sun lit up the figure of a young man in uniform. He was then in his late twenties but looked much younger. He wore an artilleryman's dress uniform which, like all the Austrian uniforms of the time, was a work of classic beauty: chocolate-brown material set off by a high stand-up collar and cuffs in bright vermilion.

Wittgenstein brought greetings from Adolf Loos, the eminent Viennese architect, who at the time was my teacher. The two had become acquainted shortly before, I believe as a result of an introduction given to Wittgenstein by Ludwig von Ficker of Innsbruck, publisher of the journal *Der Brenner*.[1] When Loos heard that Wittgenstein was due to go to Olmütz for a period of military training, he gave him my address and asked him to convey his greetings to me. My stay in Vienna and my attendance at Loos's building classes had been interrupted at the time by a prolonged illness from which I recovered at home in Olmütz.

To give a verbal description of a face – of any face that is not utterly vacuous and expressionless – so vividly that an imaginative reader or listener can actually visualize it is a task rarely if ever achieved. Therefore I will not attempt to describe Wittgenstein's appearance at the time of his stay in Olmütz but rather leave it at what little I have already said about his first visit.

4

We had only a few regular guests at our evening gatherings. Apart from my mother, Wittgenstein, and myself (but only rarely my father who spent most evenings at the coffeehouse in his circle of regulars), there were just three friends who came frequently:

Fritz Zweig, a student of music and an outstanding pianist, was also attending an artillery training course. On several

[1] See Appendix.

later occasions his wonderful piano and organ playing gave much happiness to Wittgenstein while on leave in Olmütz. Later on he was first conductor at the Berlin State Opera House. Like some other gifted conductors, but with unusual mastery, he was able to give vivid solo performances of an opera or oratorio by humming the voice parts and making the piano sound like an orchestra. In this way we were treated especially to Mozart, Schumann, Schubert, and Brahms. (Thanks to listening to these performances for years I acquired a comparatively wide knowledge of classical music, unusual for a musical layman not playing any instrument.) In our conversations we execrated Richard Wagner, that destroyer of music and culture, who at the time was still considered the pope of music and above criticism. Wittgenstein did not join in these execrations, but he did not much object either. Most sublime were Fritz Zweig's renderings of Bach's organ music (which he played to us at the synagogue when it was not in use). At the house of Fritz Zweig's parents there were regular chamber-music evenings (the violinist Gräser, later a well-known member of the Vienna Philharmonic Orchestra, was one of the participants) which Wittgenstein attended and greatly enjoyed whenever he was in Olmütz.

Fritz's cousin Max Zweig, a former classmate of mine at the *Gymnasium*, studied law in Vienna, was serving at the time in the administrative office of a military hospital, and wrote plays. After completing the studies forced upon him by his father, he devoted himself entirely to his literary pursuits. He wrote several plays in the years that followed; one of them, on St. Francis of Assisi, was performed at the *Burgtheater* in Vienna. The way in which he had uncompromisingly disregarded all other considerations and renounced the career and material advantages that were within his grasp in order to dedicate himself entirely to his artistic calling impressed even Wittgenstein, severe critic that he was in such matters. Later on Max Zweig came under the influence of the eminent critic and philosopher Paul Ernst and his theory of the strict art forms of the drama and the *Novelle*, a theory that firmly pointed the way in a time of chaos.

The third and most ebullient member of our circle was Heinrich Groag, like Max Zweig a student of law, at the time (I believe) still in civilian life; later he served in the artillery. He was the younger son of a widowed mother. He idolized his elder brother, a highly gifted young scholar (pupil of the ethnologist Luschan) who was killed in the war soon afterwards. His mother was plunged into utter despair, and the younger brother, too, was deeply affected for several years.

Heini Groag (as we called him) was one of the wittiest men I ever met. He had a malicious tongue, but his wit struck home with uncanny accuracy. He had an unusual gift for acting. While still at grammar school he wrote a letter paying homage to the Viennese actor Josef Kainz, the idol of the young theatregoers at the *Burgtheater*. In response Kainz invited the provincial schoolboy to Vienna and enabled him to enjoy several of his performances. This experience naturally had a formative influence on the young man's plans and ambitions, but in the end he decided, for his mother's sake, to study law. He was to become a successful barrister.

My brother—a man of rich and varied artistic talent who soon afterwards made a name for himself as a cartoonist in Vienna under the pseudonym of Peter Eng – also was in Olmütz in some semi-military position, but hardly ever participated in our gatherings (he also lived away from home). Wittgenstein, who in later years was to meet him socially in Vienna on a friendly footing, had in Olmütz at the time – and not without justification – a strong aversion to my brother, who returned it. Nor did Wittgenstein like his cartoons, which were very malicious and very effective.

Wittgenstein thought the draughtsmanship undistinguished, but appreciated the ingenuity of the brief captions.

For the sake of this book I deeply regret that the often devastating caricatures of Wittgenstein and the other members of the circle which my brother produced in inexhaustible quantities got lost during the Hitler period. I should have liked to use some of them as illustrations for this book, for they would recapture the whole milieu and portray above all Wittgenstein himself in a few pencil strokes far more tellingly than I can do in words. At the same time the drawings were so cynical and irreverent that a merely verbal description would seem offensive, for it was indeed only the irresistibly comical draughtsmanship that redeemed them.

The only instance I dare mention dates from a later period in Vienna, when Wittgenstein liked to visit the home of my brother and his most lovable wife, a paintress who was born in Vienna but had grown up in America. My brother had composed a short dramatic satire entitled 'An evening at the Stonboroughs' ' (Mrs. Stonborough was Wittgenstein's sister Margarete, who lived in Vienna). There Tolstoy is presented as a kind of spectacular monster under the name of 'Lew Fux Nikolajewitsch Tollhaus',[1] led like a bear on a chain. The most offensive aspect of that satire, of course, was its lampooning of Wittgenstein's ideological convictions. But when my brother read the uncensored text of the satire to the devout Tolstoy-admirer Wittgenstein – in the presence of only myself and my brother's wife – the reaction was unexpected. Wittgenstein slipped from the sofa and, shaken by spasms of uncontrollable laughter, literally rolled on the carpet. It was a grotesque scene to witness, especially from a man who normally exercised exceptional self-control. It must have been an eruption of long-pent-up psychological resistances.

As for Wittgenstein's judgement of the small circle he

[1] German for 'madhouse'.

met in my home, I remember one occasion – I believe it was at the end of his first prolonged stay in Olmütz – when he told me: 'There is intelligence there all right – enough to feed the pigs'. Now, this expression – one of the Austrian colloquialisms Wittgenstein liked to use – might easily be misunderstood. The phrase is slightly disparaging, but only in that it suggests that some stuff is available in super-abundance and therefore not particularly valuable. It says there is enough and to spare of this – even to feed the pigs; it definitely does not mean that this is good for nothing except feeding to the pigs. So Wittgenstein's judgement expresses appreciation, though not unqualified, of that plenitude of intelligence.

5

Wittgenstein, who attended the artillery training school in Olmütz as a 'one-year conscript',[1] was looking for a room. As he told me soon afterwards, his first idea – conceived presumably after seeing a few rooms and not liking the landlords – had been to lodge with the watchman of the town hall tower. This tower, 243 feet high, is a striking example of Renaissance architecture and a true emblem of the city. It must have afforded a particularly fine view over the roofs of the old fortress city and the spreading Hanna lowlands. The look-out gallery was about 170 feet up, roughly at the level of the tenth floor of a tenement building. My objection that living so high up without a lift would be too strenuous did not impress Wittgenstein. He mounted the stairs and regretted afterwards that the watchman in the tower did not want to take in a lodger.

Wittgenstein rented a furnished room in a multi-storied tenement house on the outskirts of the town on the way to the artillery range where he had to attend. Soon after the

[1] Young men who had completed secondary education to university entrance standard were excused two of the normal three years of compulsory military service.

beginning of his period of military training in Olmütz, he contracted severe enteritis and was unable to leave his room. My mother quite often cooked light food for him. The first time when – much to his surprise – I brought him his lunch, some of the brimful containers spilled over as I walked up the stairs and my shabby, old black winter coat was bespattered with thick oaten gruel. I entered; Wittgenstein was in bed. 'My dear friend', he exclaimed, 'you are showering me with kindnesses.' 'I am afraid I have been showering myself', I managed to say. Wittgenstein was highly amused.

6

The following account is meant to elucidate a passage in one of the letters (see I. 5) which otherwise would be hard to explain.

The climax of the 'season' during Wittgenstein's first stay in Olmütz was an amateur performance at the '*Palais* on the Mauritzplatz' of Molière's *Malade imaginaire*, which he attended as a delighted and high-spirited spectator. My sister – who in later years became a gifted paintress but suffered all her life from severe depression and, at the time, lived in the seclusion of her room at home, aloof from our evening gatherings – was persuaded by her women friends to accept a part, and acquitted herself very well. I myself had always been eager to try my talents as a producer. I overcame the misgivings and scruples of conscience about staging such a show while the war with all its horrors continued. I was torn by bitter inner struggles, for I was passionately drawn to a venture which my pacifist urges condemned as frivolous. I was then, as later, myself a great hypochondriac, and – as usual in such cases – it was hard to draw the borderline between my real, and by no means trifling, complaints and my imaginary ailments. The fact that Molière himself had paid with his life for his immortal satire on hypochondria and medicine (he died immediately after playing the title role) weighed, if anything, in favour of participation, and I have never regretted that our performance came off. It turned out a memorable experience, an event of some splendour in our small-town environment, and gave much happiness above all to my parents, for such satisfactions did not often come their way.

III. *Religious Matters*

'When I try to find a handy phrase summing up the period
before the first world war, in which I grew up, I hope I am
putting it most succinctly if I say: it was the golden age of
security. Everything in our Austrian monarchy which had lasted
almost a thousand years was built on permanence, and the state
itself was the supreme guarantor of that stability.' (Stefan Zweig,
The World of Yesterday, 1942)

I believe that Hitler's blind ravings about his thousand
years to come have nearly found a match in the purblind-
ness about a thousand bygone years which is reflected in
this statement by a well-known writer, who here identifies
himself with the deceptive sense of security of a generation
that had from childhood lived on the fat of the land. Otherwise he could not have failed to feel the atmosphere of
that security like a stifling noose round his neck, like the
writing on the wall, a warning that such a life simply
could not end well either for himself or for the world at
large. That this noose had stifled even the masses who had
not been quite so fortunate is proved to me by the brief
outburst of mass enthusiasm at the beginning of the war
in summer 1914. I myself was carried away at the time, and
I am not ashamed of it to this day.

Young people reacted in different ways to the atmosphere
of the pre-war era. Some accepted that sheltered ease as a
legitimate answer to their own inner needs and stresses,
others simply could not breathe in that stifling atmosphere,
which they found unbearably at variance with their spiritual
situation.

Soon after the outbreak of the war I was declared
medically fit for military service, although during my

adolescence I had spent nine months at a sanatorium with acute tuberculosis and it seemed obvious that my health could not stand up to physical hardships or exertions. We were quartered in hutments (it was November 1915, I believe), and I had to sleep from the first night on a straw mattress placed directly on the damp floor, which at once brought on a renewed attack of my pulmonary disease. After a few days I was temporarily discharged from military service and sent home.

As soon as my condition had improved I made occasional visits to Vienna, talked to Loos about continuing my studies at his school of architecture, and met Karl Kraus every evening – as I had done during earlier stays in Vienna – at the Café Pucher on the Kohlmarkt.

In the storms and raptures of general enthusiasm Kraus was one of the few who saw and comprehended. At first his scepticism could not shake my attitude. Not until the fronts in Western Galicia became stabilized and the immediate threat receded, in May 1915, did I become sufficiently open-minded to begin to do justice to his stand of complete and bitter opposition to the war. I started to help him in his work by collecting newspaper cuttings in the spirit of his subsequent book *Die letzten Tage der Menschheit* (*The Last Days of the Human Race*). On returning home after my brief visits to Vienna I continued this work for many months.

The daily reports about the frightfulness of the war – which then, after decades of peace, aroused far more horror than they do in our time – had thrown me, highly strung as I was, into a state of extreme agitation, culminating in a severe nervous crisis with weeks of near-sleeplessness.

My own situation had become morally completely untenable to me. While my contemporaries were at the front, I sat at home, an idle spectator. It was clear to me that my opposition to the war did not in itself absolve me from my moral duty of war service. I felt that here a higher call forced me to break an obligation of lesser rank, the obligation of general patriotism. At the same time the higher call categorically dictated the adoption of some other equally serious activity serving its ends.

At that time, in 1916, pacifism in its common form ventured its first, timid utterances in the countries of the Central Powers (though the statements came invariably from the neutral world outside). But this type of pacifism was always distasteful to me. It was clear to me that pacifist utterances could only claim to be serious if they sought to offer as an alternative to combatant war service some other equally serious activity involving equal physical danger.

I shall say no more about the inner struggles which, from the second year of the war, dominated my thinking and feeling for many years. This is not the place for a literary confession about my own life to readers who, after all, are interested in Wittgenstein, not myself. But I must mention a few points about this decisive issue, as they played an important part in our relationship at the time.

In those years I lived with the ever-present awareness that I was too weak to fulfil what I felt to be my most serious duties. Later I read that the British courts adopted the only right attitude towards conscientious objectors: they looked into the earlier life of the accused and asked if he had lived up to principles justifying the primacy of religious over civic duties. Only if that was the case, was he allowed to do non-combatant (but still dangerous) service.

I have never subscribed to the view that an individual's pacifist convictions wipe out his general duties to the State. I only held that there were occasions when those duties must be violated for the sake of higher ones. Nor have I ever shared the view of some humanitarian philosophers (such as Popper-Lynkeus) who consider human life the highest good in any circumstances. I felt there were things to be treasured more highly still, but that it was forbidden to destroy life for the sake of anything ranking below those supreme values.

Wittgenstein held a completely different view. He considered his duty to serve in the war as an overriding obligation. When he heard that his friend Bertrand Russell was in prison as an opponent of the war, he did not withhold his respect for Russell's personal courage in living up to his convictions, but felt that this was heroism in the wrong place.

There could be no compromise between our views. But it gave me satisfaction to see that he was convinced of my sincerity in this issue, demonstrated as it was by everything I did during the war. He did not believe in the usefulness of the action which followed of necessity from my principles. I do not propose here to describe this type of action, but may say that the effects did not remain quite as fanciful and imaginary as he, too, expected at the time.

This attitude, which remained fundamental to me, despite all my failures, was psychologically a fertile soil and stimulated impassioned thinking and re-thinking. It was the inner experience of my own inadequacy and sinfulness – felt so much more poignantly and vividly than before the war – that lifted my religion above the level of a purely literary neo-religious trend that would have repelled Wittgenstein.

To Wittgenstein his life at the front – it must have been a life of extreme danger (he never spoke a word about it) – undoubtedly was the source of deep conflicts of conscience. It was my own spiritual predicament that enabled me to understand, from within as it were, his utterances that mystified everyone else. And it was this understanding on my part that made me indispensable to him at that time.

2

When Wittgenstein had visited us in the evening I accompanied him to his room on the outskirts of the town.

73

Sometimes, if we were still engrossed in our conversation, he would in turn accompany me part of the way, or the whole way, back to my home, and our nocturnal conversations sometimes continued for two hours or so.

Our conversations might drift to any subject under the sun but centred mostly on two broad topics. There were first his attempts to explain to me the philosophical conceptions of the *Tractatus*, which made a profound impression on me. Even more important to me and (I have since come to the conclusion) at the same time considerably more interesting to him also were our talks on a second topic to which, in contrast to the first, I too was able to contribute.

My presence as a listener and my comments on his remarks mattered to him above all because the spiritual experience engendered in me by the war was giving new depth to some of my previous ideas and played a crucially important part in my life and activities.

'How glad I would be to see you again soon! Because the active use of *my reason* which your presence makes possible has *some kind of soothing effect* on me'[1] Wittgenstein once wrote to me. Now these letters and my recollections of our conversations are presented here in order to throw light on the motives that led him to write the *Tractatus*, seen in the context of his inner life at the time of completing the book. As for the problems of understanding the book as a work of logic and logically oriented philosophy, more than enough has been written in the meantime. It may be of advantage, however, to have a key to a deeper understanding of the reasons why he wrote the book.

In me Wittgenstein unexpectedly met a person who, like many members of the younger generation, suffered acutely under the discrepancy between the world as it is and as it ought to be according to his lights, but who tended also to seek the source of that discrepancy within, rather than outside, himself. This was an attitude which

[1] I. *26*. Engelmann's italics.

74

Wittgenstein had not encountered elsewhere and which, at the same time, was vital for any true understanding or meaningful discussion of his own spiritual condition.

It would be idle to reconstruct our conversations from memory. In any case it goes against the grain with me to write down afterwards what was said in a conversation, however profoundly it impressed me. On the other hand, whenever the results of our conversations became crystallized in the form of 'propositions', they were, I believe, indelibly imprinted on my mind, and I shall quote such propositions in the appropriate context. In fact, even the thoughts I am here presenting as my own – without acknowledgement of authorship – have invariably been stimulated in the course of such conversations with Wittgenstein, either during his stays on leave in Olmütz or during my repeated visits to him in later years, and they have remained the permanent foundation of my own thinking. All this, of course, cannot, and is not meant to, stand as a reliable account of his thinking, although for me it forms part of it.

In the following passages the second and more important topic of our talks is described as 'religious'. This term has a wide range of meanings and I do not want to give a hard and fast definition here. The following poem, which Wittgenstein once asked me to send him,[1] will give a much better indication of the right meaning:

> Bidden by death's sombre Angel
> Flies the Soul through depths nocturnal.
> And he leads her to the Judge.
>
> Through dread night, through sick corruption
> Eye to radiant eye they struggle:
> 'Art Thou guilty? Wilt confess?'
>
> 'Guiltless was I, guiltless am I,
> Am as my Creator made me,
> My Creator bears the guilt.'

[1] I. *8.*

75

Flung into the deepest chasm,
Ringed by tongues of angry fire
Burns the Soul and burns her pride.

And the Soul amidst Hell's fires
Says: 'Yet He, up there, has pleasure
With his Angels and he mocks me.

'Could I see Him I would spare Him
Not a spark of flames tormenting
Which I suffer free from guilt.'

Lo, a storm on wings descending
Flies into Hell's fiery furnace
And it bids the soul to come.

Leads her into highest Heaven,
Where the Angels, veiled and mourning,
Gather round the empty throne.

'Speak, where is He, veilèd Angels,
Does He shun me, is He hiding?'
'No, He burns in searing Hell.'

Then the Soul woke from her vision,
And it was a deep awakening
From the dream she dreamed in Hell.

And amid Hell's raging fire
Sang the Soul: 'What sears and burns me
Is God's love, for I have sinned.'

Sound bursts forth from all the Heavens,
And my hands are grasped by Angels,
And they cry, 'God is Almighty'.

He was on leave in Olmütz on that occasion. On the day after his arrival we went out together in the morning to be able to talk undisturbed. In a remote, and at the time of day deserted, avenue of the city park we sat down on a bench, and there, quite contrary to my custom, I read the poem to him. I must have written it not long before. As the letter confirms, it made a marked impression on him.

If I am unhappy and know that my unhappiness reflects a gross discrepancy between myself and life as it is, I have solved nothing; I shall be on the wrong track and I shall never find a way out of the chaos of my emotions and thoughts so long as I have not achieved the supreme and crucial insight that that discrepancy is not the fault of life as it is, but of myself as I am. Any attempt to put the blame on life since I 'am as my Creator made me' is mistaken because – to name only one reason – I cannot pretend that my present condition flows exclusively from a set of external circumstances permanently outside my control, including my inherited disposition. It is plain – and should be self-evident – that this is not the truth.

The person who has achieved this insight and holds on to it, and who will at least try again and again throughout his life to live up to it, is religious. He 'has the faith', from which it does not follow by any means that he must use mythological concepts – self-created or handed down – to buttress and interpret his insight into the fundamental relationship between himself and human existence in general. If he depends on such concepts in order to stand by his faith, the reason may well lie in a weakness of that faith. He should be able to stand by it without justification or explanation.

All this certainly does not imply that religion is here reduced to what is commonly described as morality.

Was Wittgenstein religious? If we call him an agnostic, this must not be understood in the sense of the familiar polemical agnosticism that concentrates, and prides itself, on the argument that man could never know about these matters.

The idea of a God in the sense of the Bible, the image of God as the creator of the world, hardly ever engaged Wittgenstein's attention (as G. H. von Wright rightly points out in his *Biographical Sketch*), but the notion of a last judgement was of profound concern to him. 'When we meet again at the last judgement' was a recurrent phrase with him, which he used in many a conversation at a

77

particularly momentous point. He would pronounce the words with an indescribably inward-gazing look in his eyes, his head bowed, the picture of a man stirred to his depths.

The key to an understanding of the many self-accusations uttered by Wittgenstein at that time and in his later school-mastering period lies in the fact that *he was not a penitent.* To cast himself in any role even remotely like it would have seemed to him a gross case of religious hypocrisy, for which he had a mortal hatred. What prompted him was an over-powering – and no doubt long-suppressed – urge to cast off all encumbrances that imposed an insupportable burden on his attitude to the outside world: his fortune as well as his necktie. The latter (I remember having been told) he had in his early youth selected with particular care, and no doubt with his unerring taste. *But he did not discard it in order to do penance* (I am sure he remembered it without any compunction). He simply had for years led a life out of harmony with all this, and so he eventually decided to shed all the things, big or small, that he felt to be petty or ludicrous. So when from that time on he went about without a tie in an open-necked shirt, he was not *donning a new garb* (say, that of a penitent); on the contrary, he was trying (unsuccessfully) to go about without any garb at all.

I have truthfully reported here what religion meant to me, at any rate in the first year of our acquaintance; what my entirely subjective and personal feelings about it were; how religion, together with art, fashioned my spiritual life during the war and for many years afterwards; and how I have striven – unsuccessfully on the whole, yet earnestly – to change my everyday life according to its demands.

Yet, I fear that this account will be misunderstood, and that in particular the image of Wittgenstein will be affected and falsified as a result. I have described his lively and deep interest in what I told him and, even more, in what he perceived himself. But in doing so, I never intended in the least to make propaganda for the feelings and thoughts that moved me at the time. I confine myself to the most essential points, so as to elucidate some passages in his letters which I consider important. First of all, to clear up some of the most likely misconceptions, a few words about how *not* to visualize Wittgenstein's attitude to religion:

Above all, he was never a mystic in the sense of occupying his mind with mystic-gnostic fantasies. Nothing was further from his mind than the attempt to paint a picture of a world beyond (either before or after death), about which we cannot speak. (He says in the *Tractatus* that the fact of a life after death could explain nothing.)

The conclusions, however, which Wittgenstein and I drew, each of us from his own religious concepts, were different, in keeping with the difference in both the magnitude and direction of our talents and abilities. He 'saw life as a task', and on that I agreed with him. Moreover, he looked upon all the features of life as it is, that is to say upon all facts, as an essential part of the conditions of that task; just as a person presented with a mathematical problem must not try to ease his task by modifying the problem. But – it may be asked – could it not be that for an individual of a suitable disposition such a modification of the data of the task may actually form *part of the task*, indeed may be felt in his conscience as vital to the task itself? Yet, the person who consistently believes that the reason for the discrepancy lies in himself alone must reject the belief that changes in the external facts may be necessary and called for.

3

Wittgenstein felt unreserved admiration and respect for Tolstoy, at least when I knew him. Among Tolstoy's writings he had an especially high regard for *The Gospel in Brief* and the Folk Tales.[1] One story is about two old Russian peasants who in fulfilment of a vow made long ago set out on a pilgrimage to Jerusalem. During the journey one of them pulls his snuff-box out of his pocket and snuffs. His companion reproaches him for such behaviour unfitting for a pilgrim. 'Sin got the better of me', the other replies.

Such self-knowledge – Wittgenstein thought – was a sign of true religious feeling: instead of trying to excuse his action before himself and others as 'not really sinful', the peasant confessed having succumbed to sin.

And often he quoted, full of enthusiasm, the words spoken by the convicted officer and libertine Dmitri Karamazov in full awareness of his guilt: 'Hail to the Highest – also within me!'[2]

In Tolstoy's tale only one of the two pilgrims, the one who admonished his friend, reaches Jerusalem. The other never got beyond a famine-stricken area in the Ukraine which they had passed on their way. There, in a miserable hovel, he found a family of cottagers starving and on the point of death. He could not tear himself away until he had saved them and nursed them back to health, spending in the process all the money he had saved up for the journey. So he returned home by himself.

The first peasant, though in Jerusalem, finds it impossible, among the bustling throngs of pilgrims and under constant threat from pickpockets, to concentrate his thoughts on devotion. At the Holy Sepulchre he sees at the head of the crowd his lost companion surrounded by a halo. But he cannot reach him.

Back home he finds his companion attending to the beehives in his garden. Lit up by a shaft of sunlight, the

[1] In the 'World's Classics' volumes entitled *A Confession etc.* and *Twenty-Three Tales* respectively. The folk tale is entitled 'Two Old Men'.

[2] *The Brothers Karamazov*, Book III, Ch. iii (actually long before Dmitri's supposed crime).

bees seem to float around his head like the halo in Jerusalem. But when the returning pilgrim tells his friend what he saw and asks about his stay with the starving, the other hushes him with some alarm: 'That is God's business, my friend, God's business. But come into the house and taste some of my honey.'

Significantly, Tolstoy chose a passage from the Gospel of St. John (IV, 19–23) as a motto for this tale. It will not be amiss, I believe, to place it at the end of this section:

'The woman saith unto him, Sir, I perceive that thou art a prophet. Our fathers worshipped in this mountain and ye say, that in Jerusalem is the place where men ought to worship. Jesus said unto her, Woman, believe me, the hour cometh, when ye shall neither in this mountain, nor yet at Jerusalem, worship the Father. Ye worship ye know not what; we know what we worship: for salvation is of the Jews. But the hour cometh, and now is, when the true worshippers shall worship the Father in spirit and in truth.'

IV. *Literature, Music, and Cinema*

The sphere of intellectual life in which I have gained most through Wittgenstein's influence, through the lasting impressions which our conversations left with me, is that of literature. As for the religious matters already discussed here, it gave me, of course, immense satisfaction that a superior mind was listening receptively and with true understanding to what I had to say about my feelings, and that he helped me to limit and correct my attitude in important aspects, Yet, to *think* about these things was not his line at all; his decisive achievement here is the demarcation of the boundary of the possibilities of verbal expression in that direction.

Conversely, his philosophy, the ideas of the *Tractatus*, went far beyond my own mental grasp and experience at the time. What was presented to me here at first hand, in matchless quality, and moreover with the immediacy of the spoken word, was irreplaceable; yet – as I was fully aware – it benefited me then only to the extent of opening a door, an opportunity of learning how to look at the world. That is what happened, and it took years until I truly understood the *Tractatus* as a whole. But then, the pursuit of philosophical insights was never one of my deepest impulses.

When Wittgenstein was working on the completion of the *Tractatus* – possibly before he had given final shape to the statement of his mystical insights – he wrote a letter (I. 6, dated 9.4.17) worth quoting again. I had sent him a poem by Uhland which is 'so clear that no one understands it' (Karl Kraus) and which, in a certain sense, touched me differently and more deeply than even the poetry –

already rediscovered at the time – belonging to the great past of German literature. He replied:

The poem by Uhland is really magnificent. And this is how it is: if only you do not try to utter what is unutterable then *nothing* gets lost. But the unutterable will be — unutterably — *contained* in what has been uttered!

The 'positive' achievement of Wittgenstein, which has so far met with complete incomprehension, is his pointing to *what is manifest in a proposition*. And what is manifest in it, a proposition cannot also state explicitly. The poet's sentences, for instance, achieve their effect not through what they say but through what is manifest in them, and the same holds for music, which also says nothing.

This is Uhland's poem:

GRAF EBERHARDS WEISSDORN[1]

Graf Eberhard im Bart
Vom Württemberger Land,
Er kam auf frommer Fahrt
Zu Palästinas Strand.

Daselbst er einmal ritt
Durch einen frischen Wald;
Ein grünes Reis er schnitt
Von einem Weißdorn bald.

Er steckt es mit Bedacht
Auf seinen Eisenhut;
Er trug es in der Schlacht
Und über Meeres Flut.

Und als er war daheim,
Er's in die Erde steckt,
Wo bald manch neuen Keim
Der milde Frühling weckt.

Der Graf, getreu und gut,
Besucht es jedes Jahr,
Erfreute dran den Mut,
Wie es gewachsen war.

Der Herr war alt und laß,
Das Reislein war ein Baum,
Darunter oftmals saß
Der Greis in tiefem Traum.

Die Wölbung, hoch und breit,
Mit sanftem Rauschen mahnt
Ihn an die alte Zeit
Und an das ferne Land.

[1] COUNT EBERHARD'S HAWTHORN

Count Eberhard Rustle-Beard,
From Württemberg's fair land,
On holy errand steer'd
To Palestina's strand.

The while he slowly rode
Along a woodland way;
He cut from the hawthorn bush
A little fresh green spray.

Then in his iron helm
The little sprig he plac'd;
And bore it in the wars,
And over the ocean waste.

And when he reach'd his home,
He plac'd it in the earth;
Where little leaves and buds
The gentle Spring call'd forth.

83

Uhland's poem came to play a part in my life. What I had learned before as a reader of Karl Kraus was here for the first time brought home to me by direct experience: the fact that poetry can produce a profound artistic effect *beyond* (but never without) the immediate effect of its language. It is true that it needs a rare and felicitous conjuncture to bring off that effect.

Like my contemporaries as a whole – and unlike the preceding generation – I had by that time (1917) acquired an understanding of the genuine poetry of the nineteenth century (in my case especially Eichendorff and Mörike). From our primary school readers I had remembered some poems by Uhland for their special purity and charm (whereas others, notably 'The Minstrel's Curse', repelled me both by their contents and by their language). Once, looking through the poems that had so far meant nothing to me, I chanced on 'Count Eberhard's Hawthorn' and was deeply moved. Something in that poem struck me as completely new: taken singly, no line had either the beauty and conspicuous depth of a verse, say, by Eichendorff ('Aus der Heimat, hinter den Blitzen rot!' – 'From home, behind the flame-cleft sky') or the unromantic verbal magic of a Mörike ('Gelassen stieg die Nacht an's Land' – 'With measured step night strode ashore'). Each one of Uhland's verses was simple – not ingenuous, but tersely informative ('On holy errand steer'd to Palestina's strand') – so that none of them, taken by itself, would

---

He went each year to it,
The Count so brave and true;
And overjoy'd was he
To witness how it grew.

The Count was worn with age
The sprig became a tree;
'Neath which the old man oft
Would sit in reverie.

The branching arch so high,
Whose whisper is so bland,
Reminds him of the past
And Palestina's strand.
(transl. by Alexander Platt, 1848)

cause delight. But the poem as a whole gives in 28 lines the picture of a life. The impression was so powerful that I understood that here was a higher level of poetry and language which had previously eluded me.

Wittgenstein's letter showed me to my delight that he shared my reaction. Naturally he grasped the matter far more deeply than I had done, and I attach immense significance to the way in which he formulated his impression. It seems to me indeed that his discovery of what a proposition cannot make explicit because it is manifest in it – in my view the essential core of the *Tractatus* although only adumbrated in the book – has found a lasting expression in this letter.

2

In an earlier letter (I. 5) Wittgenstein comments on two works by the Viennese poet Albert Ehrenstein. I should not have published this letter with its unfavourable judgement about a writer no longer with us, who was a personally attractive man (a friend of the painter Kokoschka for whom I have a high regard), if I had thought that this was merely a personal condemnation. In fact, the judgement refers to an entire literary epoch, to what was then proclaimed as expressionism and, under different names and in ever lower forms of execution, has continued to dominate literary life to this day.

Particularly revealing to me is the type of artistic effect sought by Wittgenstein as an antidote to expel the sickening taste of such poetry: he chose the most severely classical verse of Goethe and Mörike. His shock can be compared to that of a severely wounded soldier who cries out to be refreshed and, expecting to be given a sip of brandy, brings the cup to his lips, only to taste dishwater. This should not be misunderstood by assuming that Wittgenstein objects to the portrayal of human misery by art whatever the circumstances. He does not, provided it is done in the right place and – in the words of Socrates – in the 'rhythms of a decorous and manly life'.

Wittgenstein was enraptured by Mörike's immortal story, *Mozart's Journey to Prague*, and in it especially by the passages describing musical effects in words: 'Coming as from remotest starry worlds, the sounds fall from the mouth of silver trombones, icy cold, cutting through marrow and soul; fall through the blueness of the night', he would recite with a shudder of awe.

As a rule it is a bold venture indeed to attempt to re-capture in words what music has achieved. But in the rare cases where the venture succeeds, as it does here, we are in the presence of sublime peaks of poetic language, and thus of verbal expression altogether. Here was one of the great passages in literature touching on Wittgenstein's most central language problem: that of the border of the unutterable and yet somehow expressible.

And again his enthusiasm here is aroused by what is banal (in the highest sense of the word). The significance of that banality, which is closely bound up with the most central problem of the contemporary moral-aesthetic scene – that of the border between genuine and sham emotion – was discovered and discussed by Karl Kraus. (This also is Adolf Loos's problem in architecture.) And it is always and only simplicity which, if successful, hits the very centre of the target.

3

Gottfried Keller, one of the few great writers whom Wittgenstein revered wholeheartedly, indeed passionately, was superbly and exhaustively characterized by Ricarda Huch when she speaks about '*his veracity that will not permit his tone to be louder than his feeling by as much as a single vibration*'. Such veracity, matching expression with emotion, is pre-cisely what Wittgenstein was seeking in art, and it seems to me that this seeking was also the driving force of his philosophizing. If the results of the latter appear to be utterly misunderstood, it is manifestly because his readers have so far been without the master-key to its understanding, and because they are looking for its significance in all possible aspects which *I know* to have been of no or only marginal importance to him.

Lesser writers, from whom Keller is distinguished by this perfect fit between what is said and what is genuinely felt, speak in a very much louder tone that would be warranted by the real depth of their feeling. In expressing they exaggerate their emotion, and yet (as Goethe puts it in *Faust*) for all their 'ell-high buskins' and 'wigs of a million locks' they remain what they were. Now they effect such exaggeration and over-emphasis by words and phrases added to the absolute minimum of what has to be said. And Wittgenstein sees in the field of philosophy entire edifices piled up from such locks in their millions, but he does not think that these desperate attempts to catch the blue-bird of metaphysics are any more significant than the salt that you are supposed to sprinkle on the bird's tail for the same purpose.

What Wittgenstein forbids has been more than sufficiently understood. Yet no one is ready to appreciate that, unlike the positivists who so reverently misunderstand him, Wittgenstein has also allowed something – something, indeed, that had so far escaped the notice of philosophers – and that in this second act his true achievement lies. For the prohibitions are only meant to clear a path hitherto blocked: the path to that which is not stated in a proposition but is manifest in it.

4

The writing of all the writers so far mentioned was (at least in part) word-music. But Grillparzer, a truly great writer in the old classical sense, was no word-musician. Although his poetry as a whole is not among the most compelling manifestations of his personality, he has written magnificent verses (for instance in his long auto-biographical poem *Reminiscences in the Green*); but they are clearly not word-music.

One of Grillparzer's plays which particularly appealed to Wittgenstein was *A Faithful Servant of his Master*. Here the old and worthy Paladin Bancbanus is installed as Deputy to the absent King of Hungary, and demonstrates his self-sacrificing loyalty by his silent but firm resistance to the 'spurns that patient merit of the unworthy takes'.

The loyalty of a lofty spirit portrayed in this play was so incomprehensible to the educated theatre-going public even at that time (in the twenties of the nineteenth century) that the Emperor Francis (a tyrant of peasant cunning whose aunt had died under the guillotine) did not want this point mentioned in his Imperial *Burgtheater*. Accordingly he summoned the author after the successful première, and said he had liked the play so much that he wished to buy it and keep it in his sole possession – whereupon the play promptly disappeared from public view, exactly as if it had been banned by the censor.

It may appear strange that the revival of the German classics at the beginning of our century did not include Grillparzer, who has only very recently started to gain fresh recognition. Actually the reason should be obvious to those who understand the difference between creative writing and word-music, and realize that the revival was confined to those among the old classics who were also word musicians. Folk songs, Hölderlin, Eichendorff, Mörike were ready to be rediscovered as readers began to develop a deeper understanding than in the past for emotional values manifest in the language, as they began to respond to emotional values not stated in so many words.

In the first decades of the twentieth century a wave of irrationalism and glorification of sentiment – the very views against which the *Tractatus* is directed in the first place – had introduced a new variety of nonsense by plunging from one nonsense into the opposite kind. Their watchword was: 'Get rid of reason which has caused our misfortune. Let us seek salvation in feeling without reason!'

But it is not a question of head *or* heart, reason *or* emotion: the watchword must be reason *with* emotion, head *and* heart. We cannot say: what we lack is feeling. But we shall be much nearer the truth in saying: what our reason lacks is feeling, we need reason endowed with feeling, indeed with the unspoken feeling that is manifest in our reason; it is what we call heart: feeling which does not pour freely outwards in emotional self-indulgence, but which is restrained, turned inward, thus suffusing the whole personality and bringing warmth even to its coldest part, the seat of reason.

5

Wittgenstein certainly never wrote a poem in his life – not even at the age when nearly all intellectually interested young people of his generation tended to try their hand at it – because no poem ever occurred to him spontaneously. (The 'spontaneous idea' was so decisive for him that he would only recognize a philosophical proposition of his own if it had spontaneously occurred to him in the right words.) I take this to be certain, because Wittgenstein once told me that only once in his whole life had a new tune occurred to him. Yet he had a detailed knowledge of the whole range of German classical music.

When I first met him he played no instrument; later he learnt to play the clarinet, and played it very well; I once heard him in Schubert's 'Shepherd on the Rock'. Instruments apart, he whistled beautifully. On one occasion, when the conversation turned to the viola part in the third movement of a Beethoven string quartet, he whistled the part from beginning to end, with a tone as pure and strong as that of an instrument. I have repeatedly heard him perform such feats.

At the home of his sister, Mrs. Stonborough, who had rented a spacious flat in the magnificent Schönborn Palais on the Rennweg, I once witnessed a music rehearsal: one of the best-known Vienna string quartets had been invited to rehearse a piece for a later performance at the house. This was one of the first rehearsals and Wittgenstein was among the few listeners present. Extremely reserved at first, in his usual way, he started with a few modest remarks, but eventually he was carried away by passion and intervened in the rehearsal. The musicians at first reacted with gentle irony, as they presumably took the unimpressive-looking youth in his threadbare uniform (he continued to wear his service tunic for a considerable time after the war) for a conceited dilettante – whom they did not treat as curtly as they might since he happened to be a brother of their high-ranking hostess.

But I also witnessed a later rehearsal where Wittgenstein, now completely accepted by the four musicians, did most of the talking, and his objections and advice were heard as deferentially as if Gustav Mahler himself had interrupted their rehearsal.

I have experienced similar scenes in other fields where Wittgenstein acted in the same way. Invariably those concerned realized very soon that they were presented with an opportunity to learn too important to miss. But whenever he was not *completely* sure of his ground, he would not open his mouth.

6

Norman Malcolm relates that Wittgenstein was very fond of detective stories, and once said: 'How people can read *Mind* if they could read Street & Smith[1] beats me'. But the majority of his readers will take such a remark for

[1] American detective magazines.

irony, or at least for a strong ironical exaggeration of an actual dislike. If only they could imagine just how genuine this dislike was, and how anything but exaggerated its expression in such a statement! A man of his discernment had to react to any intellectual pretence with insuperable revulsion.

He did indeed greatly enjoy reading good detective stories, while he considered it a waste of time to read mediocre philosophical reflections. His taste for detective stories belongs to a later period. But during our joint work on the building of a house in the Kundmanngasse, Wittgenstein, in the same spirit, went often to the cinema to see Wild West films.

Wittgenstein had read with keen interest Tolstoy's book, *What is Art?*, and agreed with some of its conclusions. Tolstoy there argues that European art of recent centuries has been doomed to remain ineffective, because it was not intelligible to all and thus failed to give something to the 'poor in spirit' as well as to the educated. As an example of a true and perennial work of art he mentions the Old Testament story of Joseph and his brothers, which, he says, will produce the same effect on the Russian peasant as on the Russian intellectual or, for that matter, on the Chinese peasant.[1] During the last years of his life Tolstoy placed great hopes in the development of the cinema, then in its infancy. Full of enthusiasm he pointed out the opportunities of conveying through the cinema to the masses the profound spiritual effects formerly produced by art. We know today that the film has indeed a tremendous mass effect, only in a vastly different way than Tolstoy had wished.

Wittgenstein, too, considered that the cinema had great potentialities, even for *good*, but he visualized them with more realism and less naïveté than Tolstoy. When I worked with him on the house in the Kundmanngasse, we went often

[1] Chapter X (pp. 177 ff. in the 'World's Classics' edition).

in the evening to a cinema in one of the outlying districts, where Wild West films were shown which were not refined enough for the public of the superior cinemas. In these films (the world-renowned hero then was Tom Mix) the plot always culminated in a wild chase after the villain, victory of the good, liberation of the kidnapped girl, happy ending. To Wittgenstein all this constituted a similarity to the genuine fairy tale as the acting out of a wish-fulfilment dream.

What he found here had nothing to do with an educational purpose but was pure enjoyment, a spiritual release which art has ceased to offer today. The fulness of this experience was vitally dependent on the element of audience participation such as the theatre had offered in olden days, and without which it had soon become moribund. It depended on the crowd's active and enthusiastic response to the happenings on the stage (or, here, the screen) in this collective art form where the two elements must interact to ensure the complete impact.

Grillparzer at the height of his fame refused to let his last plays go on the stage because 'the audience has ceased to exist'. Much earlier in his career he had written that to him 'as a dramatist the uninhibited eruption of a crowded theatre was always ten times as interesting, and indeed instructive, as the critical lucubrations of some physically and spiritually crippled literary matador' (a remark aimed at the theatre critic Saphir who at that time dragged everything that was successful as well as genuine into the mud).

The advent of the sound film put an end to Wittgenstein's interest in this primitive but genuine branch of the arts. In our technological age the development of great new manifestations of culture is reduced to a few years, before they are killed and superseded by the next 'improvement'. But in this case those few years had sufficed to allow new forms of artistic expression to take shape.

Again and again Wittgenstein emphasized the significance of the 'happy ending'. To make a film without a happy ending, he thought, was to misunderstand the fundamentals of the cinema. Carrying the argument further, he said it was the essence of art in general to lead to a positive conclusion. The film in particular was to him the acting out of a wish-fulfilment dream and therefore, if true to form, bound to end with the gratification of desire.

This may be correct as far as the cinema is concerned, but as a universal maxim about the essence of a work of art it seems paradoxical at a first glance. Yet the maxim can be interpreted at a deeper level in the sense of Hölderlin's distichs on Oedipus:

Many have failed to find words for highest joy's joyous expression,
Here we find it at last, here in sorrow expressed.

Here the *tragic* conclusion (seemingly the opposite of the happy ending), the victory of man's loftiest aspirations over the base side of his nature, a victory he can attain and seal only through his own death, is described as 'highest joy'. In this sense the very consummation of tragedy can be felt as a happy ending, though only by the noble mind or the crowd temporarily under his sway.

The basic idea behind this view, it seems to me, is that art must always, in one sense or another, lead to a *solution*; the individual work of art, then, is an example demonstrating such a solution.

V. *Observations on the* TRACTATUS

At the time of his first stay in Olmütz Wittgenstein suffered from a minor defect of speech which, however, disappeared later on. He used to struggle for words, especially when he was trying hard to formulate a proposition. Often enough I was able to help him to find the right words by stating myself the proposition he had in mind. I could do it because I really had a sensitive understanding for what he wanted to say. More than once on such occasions he exclaimed with relief, 'If I can't manage to bring forth a proposition, along comes Engelmann with his forceps and pulls it out of me!' It is the recollection of that ability of my youth that has given me the courage to comment in these remarks, which may give little satisfaction to a philosopher, on a body of ideas that has influenced my own thinking.

To the ordinary reader, even if versed in philosophy, Wittgenstein's basic thoughts, as stated in the *Tractatus Logico-Philosophicus*, often seem incomprehensible, because 'too complex'. That they are not; but they are incomprehensible owing to the absence of the psychological conditions from which alone such thinking can spring and which must exist, though to a lesser degree, in the reader's mind as well.

Therefore the following pointers to the significance of his principal work may be useful to many readers, including those trained in philosophy. In fact I have to make these points before I can comment on the contents of the book. An understanding of the author's intention seems to me the only key to the understanding of the book.

Wittgenstein's educational career was most unusual

for a philosopher, for it was only as a mature thinker who had learnt to think quite unphilosophically in other fields of knowledge that he made (through Bertrand Russell)[1] his first acquaintance with theories of logic. This gave him as an original mind an inestimable advantage over his fellows. While still at school Wittgenstein had shown exceptional technical gifts; for instance he built model aircraft in which he anticipated problems of much later development.[2] But philosophical thinking of any sort was far from his mind at that time.

As an outsider who had learnt to think for himself he entered into discussions which would have left any other student as confused as the callow young student in Goethe's *Faust* who is overawed by Mephisto's ironical description of academic wisdom. Here the youthful Goethe, drawing on his personal experience, put the problem of academic education at the centre of his autobiographical writing. The entire first scene in the study is an accurate and merciless satirical thrust delivered by a true genius against that academic education which he, and his disciple Schopenhauer after him, considered one of the main sources of the constantly growing intellectual abasement of mankind ('the darkness of our age', as Wittgenstein put it later).[3] – One of the main roots of the evil, incidentally, is the average teacher's habit of riding the hobby-horse of his own specialized interests, leaving the unprepared student in a state of hopeless confusion from which even a mind like Wittgenstein's could not have found a way out and to the heart of the matter, had he entered the subject unprepared.

[1] Wittgenstein may have read Russell first but seems to have met Frege first (G. H. von Wright, *Biographical Sketch*, p. 5).
[2] A similar story is told about Wittgenstein's Manchester period (1908-11). See the note by Mr. W. Mays in *Mind*, lxiv (1955), pp. 247 f.
[3] In the introduction to *Philosophical Investigations*.

If we are to understand this author and his book, the following point seems particularly important to me: Wittgenstein was stimulated to write the *Tractatus* by his study of the works of Frege and Russell who, together with the physicist Heinrich Hertz, can be regarded as his principal teachers. But Wittgenstein's system of thought, born of deep personal experience and conflicts and setting out by entirely original methods to present a comprehensive philosophical picture of the world, diverges in some points from the logical systems conceived by those teachers, the founders of modern logic. As a result of such divergencies special attention came to be focused on those particular elements in the rational exposition of that complex pattern of mystical experience which were at the same time corrections of errors made by those teachers, whom Wittgenstein held in such high esteem. (Russell, according to his own statements, has accepted these corrections, at least in part.) Yet we do not understand Wittgenstein unless we realize that it was philosophy that mattered to him and not logic, which merely happened to be the only suitable tool for elaborating his world picture.

This the *Tractatus* accomplishes in sovereign fashion, ending up with implacable consistency by nullifying the result, so that the communication of its basic thoughts, or rather of its basic tendency – which, according to its own findings, cannot on principle be effected by direct methods – is yet achieved indirectly. He nullifies his own world picture, together with the 'houses of cards' of philosophy (which at that time at least he thought he had made collapse), so as to show '*how little is achieved when these problems are solved*'. What he wants to demonstrate is that such endeavours of human thought to 'utter the unutterable' are a hopeless attempt to satisfy man's eternal metaphysical urge.

How little the meaning of the *Tractatus* is understood can be seen from a remark in a *Dictionary of Philosophy* (by

Dagobert Runes)[1], which says that in the last part of his book Wittgenstein had arrived at 'certain mystical conclusions' from his views on logic. One can see the writer of this passage shake his head in shocked surprise that a Wittgenstein, having established himself as a thinker to be reckoned with, should in the end have fallen prey to such nebulous subjectivism. But irrespective of the process of growth of this system of thought, logic and mysticism have here sprung from one and the same root, and it could be said with greater justice that Wittgenstein drew certain logical conclusions from his fundamental mystical attitude to life and the world. That he should have chosen to devote five-sixths of his book to the logical conclusions is due to the fact that about them at least it is possible to speak.

A whole generation of disciples was able to take Wittgenstein for a positivist because he has something of enormous importance in common with the positivists: he draws the line between what we can speak about and what we must be silent about just as they do. The difference is only that they have nothing to be silent about. Positivism holds – and this is its essence – that what we can speak about is all that matters in life. *Whereas Wittgenstein passionately believes that all that really matters in human life is precisely what, in his view, we must be silent about.* When he nevertheless takes immense pains to delimit the unimportant, it is not the coastline of that island which he is bent on surveying with such meticulous accuracy, but the boundary of the ocean.

Now his 'mystical conclusions' are these: 'The sense of the world must lie outside the world' (6.41) (yet he does not doubt that there is such a sense – a doubt which lies at the heart of the modern mood of shiftlessness and insecurity).

'*In* it no value exists – and if it did exist it would have

[1] p. 337, s.v. Wittgenstein.

no value' (6.41) (yet that which endows things with the value which they have, which they show, is therefore simply not *in* the world. – To all these comments one must add Wittgenstein's 'but that cannot be said').

'How the world is is completely irrelevant for the sublime.[1] God does not reveal himself *in* the world' (6.432) (yet he reveals himself *through* the world, *in that* the world exists).

'There is indeed that which is unutterable. This makes itself *manifest*, it is the mystical'[2] (6.522) (but not a 'bluish haze surrounding things' and giving them an interesting appearance [as Wittgenstein once said in conversation]).

This is his one and ever-recurring thought: that the higher sphere, values, God do not form part of the contents of the world, are not something *within* the world, to be found in it and proved to exist (not something, then, which the things, the facts, the world *say*): but are something manifested *by* the world seen from outside.

No matter whether the attempt made by Wittgenstein in the *Tractatus* is a success or a failure, the decisive significance of the book, I believe, remains unaffected. It consists in having established the irrefutable separation between the higher sphere, which exists, and its expression, which is problematical, and in having shown up the fundamental dubiousness of such expression.

And an understanding of this philosopher will encourage the true believer to be undismayed in face of the advancement of enlightenment and science, however successful they may be in their proper field: because their range stops short where that which alone matters to him begins. How, indeed, could anyone believe that a work like the *Tractatus* could have been written by a man with a talent confined to

[1] Pears & McGuinness: 'How things are in the world is a matter of complete indifference for what is higher.'

[2] Pears & McGuinness: 'There are indeed things that cannot be put into words. They *make themselves manifest*. They are what is mystical.'

logic? Actually its author was a man of outstanding ability in nearly all fields of intellectual activity, 'irrational' as well as 'rational'. His aesthetic and ethical-religious insights would probably have proved far superior to the contemporary 'irrational' academic literature, and would have exerted no less influence if set out in a philosophical work than the *Tractatus* has actually exerted on logico-philosophical literature. But he believed – rightly – that the essential points on these questions had already been made, though implicitly, in the *Tractatus*.

2

The *Tractatus* is not a treatise on the nature of human language, which is regarded here merely as a special case of the more comprehensive logical category of *depiction*. Whereas Kant's theory of knowledge centres on 'reason', considered as the essential attribute of *human* thinking, the *Tractatus* focuses instead on 'language', but in such a way – and this constitutes the decisive step towards its novel way of thinking – that everything 'said' about language applies to any possible language, even a transhuman one (should such exist), so long as it is a mode of depiction.

I find nothing more instructive in this respect than his meticulous avoidance of all psychologistic thinking. So consistent was he at the time of writing the *Tractatus* in upholding this principle that even expressions which had always been tools of psychology are avoided, because the use of any such term with its encumbrance of historical connotations would of necessity have prejudged the result of the investigation. One of the very few corrections written by hand into the original typescript of the *Tractatus*[1]

[1] This typescript is in my possession. Wittgenstein gave it to me. P.E.—Through the generosity of Mr. Engelmann's friends it is now hoped to deposit this typescript in an English library.

deletes the decisive sentence 'We conceive facts in pictures' ('Die Tatsachen begreifen wir in Bildern'), and substitutes 'We make for ourselves pictures of the facts' (2.1).[1]

This may seem exaggerated, but can be likened to the surgeon's painstaking care in keeping his instruments clean. And as the surgeon knows that this may be a matter of life or death for his patient, so Wittgenstein knows that the success of all his philosophical endeavours may hinge on the choice of terms.

Modern thinking has been *infected* by psychology. This explains the need for the method of thought of the *Tractatus* which is not only free from psychology but anti-psychologistic. Despite some affinities, Wittgenstein's method is therefore different in kind, and represents a decisive step forward, from previous attempts by other thinkers who had also, and presumably from similar motives, pinned their main hope on logical thinking.

The best way to approach an understanding of the *Tractatus* – and one that leads *in medias res* – is the way that Wittgenstein himself, steeped in these thoughts as he then was, took, almost as a matter of course, in the conversations at the start of our acquaintance. I shall try to follow the same way as much as possible, especially as it was completely successful, on that first occasion, in introducing an outsider to the subject. For on that basis I was able later on, when I no longer had the benefit of his verbal explanations, to arrive, largely by my own efforts, at an understanding of the latter sections of the book which had eluded me at the time of our personal contact.

On one side stands the world, on the other side language.

'*The world is all that is the case*' (1). I.e.: If I ask a pupil, 'What are the *elements* of which the world is composed, from which it is built up?', and he understands the question, he is likely to reply: 'The world is composed of objects such as trees, houses, human beings, tables; and all objects

[1] Pears & McGuinness: 'We picture facts to ourselves'.

together are the world.' But this is not correct. It is the mark of an element, a structural component, that the world can be reconstituted from such building blocks; but a collection of objects is insufficient for this purpose. For without a knowledge of the combinations which relate objects to one another, no reconstruction, however imperfect, can be effected. In reality the table only occurs in combinations, as in the propositions: 'The table stands in the room', or 'The carpenter has made the table', etc. It is not the table, then, but the table's standing in the room, which is one of the elements constituting the world. Such an element is a *fact*. '*What is the case – a fact – is the actuality*[1] *of states of things*' (2). A state of things is a constellation of objects. And a state of things that actually obtains (is not merely possible) is a fact. The table's standing in the room (rather than, say, in the kitchen) is a state of things. If it really stands there, the state of things becomes a fact.

So much about the world. Now let us turn to the other side, that of language: As states of things are elements of the world, so propositions are the elements of language. *A proposition is an image of a fact*. A proposition is a description of a state of things, an image of an element of the world.

A proposition is composed of words (names), as the state of things (and the fact) is composed of objects. The words of the proposition form a constellation analogous to that of the constituent objects of the fact concerned, and *thereby* produce an image of that fact.

A word, or name, is not the image of an object, it is merely a sign standing for an object. But the proposition is an image of the depicted constellation of objects.

An image, a picture, can represent anything except its own representational relationship to the depicted subject. (The rays of projection from the points of the original to those of the image cannot themselves appear in the picture.) If, then, the true propositions form a picture of the world,

[1] Pears & McGuinness: 'existence' (*Bestehen*).

they can say nothing about their own relation to the world, by virtue of which they are its picture.

But this is precisely what philosophy endeavours to speak about; it seeks to set out the relationship between language and the world. It is on this point in particular, which is the subject-matter of the theory of knowledge, that Wittgenstein succeeded during his first stay in Olmütz in opening my mind to the decisive insight.

Now, this unstatable relationship between language and the world constitutes logic. ('There are no propositions of logic.'[1]) Here lies the reason why Wittgenstein's philosophical investigation is a logical one in contrast to the epistemological attempts of traditional philosophy, which are at bottom psychological, whether they admit it or not. For they treat that relationship between language and the world as part of the processes of human thought, whereas the impossibility of stating that relationship springs from the logical relation of image to original which obtains between thoughts and propositions on the one hand and the facts of reality on the other.

A proposition depicts *something* (that is, a state of things).

The 'grammatical rule' of its application is that it depicts something *outside itself*. It is applied in that sense, as something directed outwards.

Yet, one '*can*' also apply the proposition to itself, and try to depict it in its turn.

One '*can*' do that, just as one can walk on one's hands and stand on one's head, though this is contrary to the '*grammar*', as it were, of hands, feet and head.

We '*can*' of course do such a thing by way of experiment, to see what happens, and the result may be interesting for some specialized branch of knowledge. But what we must not do is to generalize the result and derive from it new

[1] Not a quotation from the *Tractatus*, which, except perhaps at 4.461, allows propositions of logic: cf. 6.12. It does, however, regard the relationship between language and the world as unstatable: cf. 2.172, 4.041, 4.12, etc.

rules of grammar about those modes of behaviour. Yet this is precisely what is involved in the attempt to evaluate such an experiment philosophically.

A man standing on his head sees the world differently from one standing on his feet. The results of such experiments need to be rectified in the light of common sense (that is, human experience dating from time immemorial). If they are generalized without such rectification, they lead to nonsense and, if adopted as norms of human behaviour, to insanity with potentially catastrophic consequences.

If the elementary facts are known, all the possible composite facts follow. The logical relations between facts are depicted by corresponding relations between the propositions. Composite propositions can be built up from elementary propositions by means of the so-called logical constants. These logical constants are represented by words such as 'and', 'or', 'if', 'not', which constitute a fundamentally different kind of word from the rest. This does not become apparent in ordinary language, because such words figure like others in a proposition; but in reality they figure in a proposition only as signs of operations to be effected with the propositions. These signs serve to turn what Wittgenstein called 'elementary propositions' into complex propositions. 'It is raining' is an elementary proposition, 'It is not raining' a complex proposition, derived from the former by the use of the logical constant 'not'.

'My fundamental idea is that the "logical constants" do not stand for anything; that nothing can stand for the *logic* of facts' (4.0312).[1]

The earlier sections of the *Tractatus* were needed to convey that fundamental idea. One of Wittgenstein's reasons for

[1] Pears & McGuinness: 'My fundamental idea is that the "logical constants" are not representatives; that there can be no representatives of the *logic* of facts.'

calling it fundamental was no doubt the great importance of this idea for the entire range of problems treated by him.

Let us imagine that hitherto unknown hieroglyphics left behind by an extinct people are discovered. Suppose further that ten of these signs are found to represent the ten figures of the decimal system, and that two further signs, at first eluding analysis, turn out to be simply the plus and minus signs. The two latter will then, in contrast to the other ten signs, 'not designate', or rather they 'designate' in a completely different manner something that lies outside the series of the other designated objects and must be kept apart from their designations.

Thus, according to Wittgenstein's insight, the logical constants do not designate any contents of reality. That is, whereas other signs have objects to which they correspond, no such correspondence attaches to the signs 'and', 'not', etc., which designate logical operations applied to the rest of the material – just as the plus and minus signs indicate similar operations applied to the ten number signs.

What happens when I 'negate' a proposition? Linguistically I can only do it by first 'drawing' the state of things to be denied just as accurately as if I meant to uphold it, and then rubbing the drawing out by the addition of the logical constant 'not' (thus I can convey the state of things, 'The book does *not* lie on the table', by first drawing a table with a book lying on it, and then rubbing out that picture by means of the logical constant 'not').

These logical constants, which play such a significant part in modern logic, are closely related to the not purely logical but transcendental-logical 'categories' which play a similar part in the older philosophical systems. Kant whose *Critique of Pure Reason* is basically a theory of categories as the fundamental regulative principles of human thought ('reason'), rectifies the list of categories laid down by Aristotle and substitutes his own table of categories. To him they are the fundamental synthetic a priori concepts of scientific thinking – basis and fountain-head of all other a priori concepts.

Now traditional philosophical opinion will grant that the elementary proposition presents a picture of a fact. But it will insist that the more complex propositional forms (and language, after all, does not consist of elementary propositions in their primary form) are capable of representing supra-empirical states of affairs and not only situations that do, or could, exist in reality. And here is the crucial point of Wittgenstein's views: according to him, complex propositional forms are merely functions of simple propositions, and therefore cannot express anything not already stated by the latter. The existence of causal or teleological relations between the facts, however, transcends the realm of facts and cannot, therefore, be expressed in meaningful propositions.

This is what Wittgenstein seeks to demonstrate by investigating the construction of complex propositional forms out of elementary propositions.

It is found that the possibilities of doing this are confined by two boundaries: on the one side that of contradiction, on the other that of tautology. Between these two limiting cases – which are not themselves meaningful propositions – extends the domain of meaningful propositions. And these alone can present a true or false, but in either case meaningful, picture of states of things.

A tautology is not a meaningful proposition (i.e. one with a content); yet it can be an indispensable intellectual *device*, an instrument that can help us – if used correctly in grasping reality, that is in grasping facts – to arrive at insights difficult or impossible to attain by other means.

Mathematics, according to Wittgenstein, is a method of logic, and – like all logical propositions – its expressions are tautologies. Logic *enables* meaningful propositions to be stated, but there are no meaningful propositions of logic itself. Mathematics constitutes a method that does not teach us anything new about the content of propositions. What it does teach us is to manipulate expressions by substitution in such a way as to throw their structure into relief and to cast it in the desired form, which was latent in the original meaningful proposition.

Mathematics consists of equations. A mathematical tautology ('equation') shows up the equivalence of different expressions (say 2×2 on the one side, 4 on the other), thus enabling them to be mutually substituted, to be interchanged in any proposition without changing the truth-value. By applying a series of successive substitutions of that kind, it is possible to obtain in the end a self-evident (i.e. intuitive) result.

It is possible, then, by means of these operations, involving no more than such interchanges of expressions, to arrive at final forms of expression which are psychologically more effective than the original expressions in revealing a pattern of relationships. This is precisely what constitutes the value of mathematics to science.

3

Wittgenstein carefully refrained in the *Tractatus* from referring directly to the history of philosophy; he even avoided, for the same reasons, any explicit mention of the traditional problems of philosophy. I must therefore ask the reader's indulgence if I here propose to follow a different course and bring other philosophical trends into the discussion.

Wittgenstein, we know, had only a very limited interest in academic philosophical literature, whether contemporary or classical. Remembering his great and often excessive conscientiousness, the compulsive thoroughness with which he surveyed any theme that occupied him, it clearly follows that, whenever he did read such literature, he found that it had little or nothing to give him. Therefore he did not feel any obligation whatever to scan those books

in order to ascertain whether their ideas agreed or con-
flicted with his own. When some passage from philosophical literature was quoted or related to him, he would
often say with utter seriousness and genuine modesty:
I do not understand it. He would first have had to delve
laboriously into the text, trying to find in the thought of
others parallels with his own at an expenditure of mental
energy which he was not prepared to sink into what to
him seemed an irrelevant effort.

For centuries metaphysics has fought rearguard actions
against advancing natural science. One after another it
was forced to surrender positions once considered im-
pregnable, and today endeavours to save it are concentrated
on the establishment of a Maginot Line designed to protect
the humanities, and thus metaphysics as well, against the
infiltration of the scientific 'positivist' attackers. Nothing
has been left untried to persuade us that the approaches
and methods of natural science are not valid in the
humanities, nor indeed – a kind of defence in depth – in the
outlying buffer zones of psychology and even biology. Even
the questioning of fundamentals by modern physics is seized
upon in these quarters as a ground for hope that the attacker
may have to beat a retreat in the heart of his own territory.

Wittgenstein himself divines and treasures the presence of
the values which are at stake here and which it is right to
protect; but he is against Maginot Lines, which he con-
siders futile. He sees those values in the 'unutterable', and
that begins behind every scientific proposition in any
branch of natural or humanistic studies (although the
danger of their destruction is more acute in the latter than
in the former). He does not draw his boundary across the
field of human knowledge as a barrier between humanistic
and natural sciences, but behind the entire field as a line
dividing all that is in any way utterable from the unutterable. Indeed, his effort is directed against philosophy's
undertaking to protect the unutterable by uttering it.

In its endeavours to rescue the 'higher sphere' (that is, values which are vital also to human society) from the threat posed by the development of science, modern philosophy seeks to smuggle such values into the universe of discourse by postulating 'higher' propositional forms (Kant's synthetic a priori judgements and the principles and postulates of pure reason) supposed to derive in principle from a different and more sublime source than the propositions originating in the lower realm of the senses, of empirical knowledge, and therefore incapable of expressing the sublime. Kant's examples of such 'higher' propositions are taken from mathematics. Now Wittgenstein contends that these propositions are truth-functions of empirical propositions, that, as limiting forms of propositions (tautologies), they are empty of content and cannot therefore state anything about either empirical or transcendental reality. Further examples refer to the so-called synthetic a priori principles of natural science, but these in turn are no more than arbitrary, more or less practical rules and do not constitute meaningful scientific propositions.

The dismissal of synthetic a priori propositions in natural science as meaningless entails the final destruction of the last tenuous bridge from the insight of theoretical reason to the principles of practical reason. Kant, it is true, denies the existence of such a bridge; yet, by seeking to formulate a supreme ethical norm in the form of a proposition, and by admitting a practical 'reason' that operates through procedures analogous to those of theoretical reason, he must be held to have re-erected it. In Wittgenstein's work the bridge is finally demolished; all those, therefore, who have considered *that* bridge the *only* access to the 'higher sphere', would then indeed be debarred from it.

The practical result of this view of the impossibility of speaking about values is the opposite of what might be expected from a cursory consideration of the problem.

Conditioned by the interpretations of liberal theologians and philosophers who seek to mediate between religion and science by pouring water into the wine until nothing but water remains, we should guess that the new view, saying that the higher values should not even be *talked* about, must lead to an ethical-religious nihilism, saying that therefore what ethics bids us do need no longer be done. But Wittgenstein implies that it ought to be done, and done most rigorously, in full measure, without any watering down, even though the authority of theories now recognized as untenable can no longer be invoked in justification.

Like all great new systems of philosophy, Wittgenstein introduces only a single, one might say 'small', modification – but it is a fundamental one. And each modification of that type entails the most far-reaching consequences for *all* branches of knowledge. It is meaningless, he says, to talk about the sphere of the transcendental, the metaphysical; and he rests this statement on a strong logical foundation. In this way he renders all attacks on the transcendental impossible, but at the same time he also frustrates all attempts to defend it by talking. Yet he adumbrates another way by which this can be done.

Here the sublime emerges not only pure, but also naked, as it were. As a layer of cloud softens as well as obscures the sunlight, so the veil woven from our weaknesses has protected us from the burning ray of the pure light. But now one feels at times lifted not merely above the clouds but into space beyond the atmosphere, where, science has it, a much hotter sun burns in a black sky.

This led to an attitude to life that comes nearest perhaps to that sought by Tolstoy: an ethical totalitarianism in all questions, a single-minded and painful preservation of the purity of the uncompromising demands of ethics, in agonizing awareness of one's own permanent failure to measure up to them. This is the demand Wittgenstein makes on himself. But even the example of a life lived in this way was sometimes apt to confuse weaker spirits, which, considered in terms of ethics, was their fault, not his.

It is clear that such an ethics is not even debatable as a general guiding line for human action. Yet ethics pre-supposes universal validity. And a 'higher' ethics for the select must be rejected, particularly from Wittgenstein's point of view.

The view of the *Tractatus* in this respect can be summed up briefly by saying: ethical propositions do not exist; ethical action does exist.

The real achievement of the *Tractatus*, as I see it, can be put in these terms:

Even *if* language were nothing but a depiction of sensually perceptible reality together with the conclusions obtained from it by abstraction, and if accordingly it were impossible to speak in any language about the higher sphere (as science and a philosophy conducted by scientific means are indeed *unable* to do) – even then there *exists* the higher sphere, there is a *sense* in our existence, there exists that from which values derive their value (and which confers it on them 'from outside the world').

The paradox thus stated is in no way weakened, but rather confirmed, by Wittgenstein's paradox of the ladder: even his own attempt at an explanation, together with the so-called mysticism of the final propositions of the *Tractatus*, is meaningless as an exposition because it is, of necessity, presented in propositions, statements of scientific form.

Any application of 'There is' in fictitious propositions such as 'There is, indeed, a higher sphere' is inadequate, and yet it makes a valid point, though by means of a logically untenable statement.

I see the essence of Wittgenstein's *Tractatus* in the follow-ing elements:

On the one hand : In the impossibility of reproducing the relationship between image and original or that between simple and complex propositions; in the consequent inability of propositions to state these relationships, though they make them 'manifest'; and hence in the impossibility of a philosophy that sets out to express those relations in meaningful propositions.

And *on the other hand* : In the analogous impossibility of uttering emotion instead of allowing it to become manifest in something that *is* utterable; and hence in the art of forgoing the utterance of emotion and expressing instead the *thought* in which it is manifest.

This shows us the nature of the deepest interconnection: *As on the one hand* the unutterable lies in the relations between language and the world ('the outside world'), *so on the other hand* does it lie in the relation between language and the world of intuitive values.

4

I believe it was during a tram ride into town from the Olmütz railway station that Wittgenstein told me he had now for the first time read the Latin version of the Bible, the Vulgate. He was enthusiastic. Only here, he said, had the text revealed to him its true shape and greatness. I understood precisely what he meant: in contrast with versions such as the German or the Greek (the Hebrew original he was unable to read) in which the emotions accompanying the rational text are conveyed with much greater immediacy, Latin is the language where reason dominates and *all* emotional aspects become manifest without words. As a result the text assumes in that language a different and new, monumental stature akin to the mode of expression Wittgenstein himself endeavoured to achieve in the *Tractatus*.

(Incidentally, on the subject of Bible translations: Much later, in Vienna, I once read to him some specimen passages of the Buber-Rosenzweig translation into German. In my view this version does unnecessary violence to the German language in places, whereas I have always had the highest respect for Luther's translation as a work of literature which reproduces the spirit of the original no less faithfully in the garb of its own time than do Rembrandt's etchings. Wittgenstein agreed with me on the whole, but judged Buber's translation somewhat more favourably than I, as he felt that in spite, or possibly because, of the liberties taken with the German language it conveyed to him the exotic and 'barbaric' aspect of the original text. This amounts to a recognition, though qualified, of the value of that translation. The term 'barbaric' was not meant disparagingly, but as a tribute to the ancient, oriental, and to us strangely exotic greatness of an archaic period of human history. The twentieth century, of course, tends to overrate all that is archaic, unlike the nineteenth century with its 'Victorian' standards. Egyptian and Babylonian art is a case in point, though one has to admit the outstanding quality of that art, beside which even a Phidias looks almost like a Hellenistic epigone. Perhaps the twenty-first century will again have a more balanced judgement in this as in other matters.)

We must guard against misunderstanding Wittgenstein's attitude to his own work, as shown in some of his letters. Schopenhauer said that it was impossible for a man six foot tall not to know that he overtopped the average, and that the same was true for intellectual stature. When Wittgenstein therefore chose his particular way of writing his book and the particular form in which it was cast, and when his thoughts and comments about the book appear self-deprecatory, it was certainly not because of any tendency to consider his book inferior to other works. His genuine 'modesty' in this respect stems from his scale of values: within the field of intellectual creation as a whole he attached little importance to any philosophical work. He wanted his book accepted as a businesslike exposition of his thoughts; accordingly he strove after a stark simplicity of style and presentation. Thus he dropped the division into chapters and substituted his own method of subdivision based on the incomparably higher structural principle of numbering in decimal notation. In this way each proposition is assigned its precise position within the whole, and the consistent arrangement of the propositions according to logical rank constitutes an unsurpassed ordering system. Nevertheless, it is a system that can scarcely be imitated, not only because of the enormous amount of intellectual work that goes into its application, but also because it is exceedingly rare for any writer to be able to think so consistently for so long a stretch. Wittgenstein himself regrets in the preface to the *Investigations* that he had not been able in writing his second work to produce sequences of thought in similarly systematic order (which, incidentally, would have been out of character with the nature of the book and its mode of thinking).

The besetting sin of false artistic endeavour is the striving to avoid banality and its odium, thus setting oneself apart from one's fellows. Invariably the frantic attempts to find striking and precious phrases lead up to falsification of the second degree, when something banal not born of personal experience is picked up at second hand, because it looked so exquisite in its original setting. (Such artificial banality is aptly described by the sarcastic use of the word 'plain', in German '*schlicht*'.) It is falsification by means of the genuine.

It will be noted again and again that the subjects – both in life and literature – which aroused Wittgenstein's attention and became problems for his thought were precisely those which the 'educated' tend to look upon as the most banal and least problematical. The intellectual interests of such people can best be compared to the appetite of a man living on the wrong sort of diet: his palate can only taste spices, sugar, and salt, so they alone are interesting to him, while he has lost all ability to distinguish the more subtle flavours of the unseasoned main ingredients of the food. Yet this, metaphorically speaking, is the field where all the problems lie that can seriously engage a genuine thinker.

This is also the reason why most of the crucial steps in the intellectual sphere are taken so late. Indeed, the man who is to make such a step must have preserved the capacity to wonder at the everyday 'banalities' dismissed by those mediocre minds as obvious and no longer worthy of note; he finds only where others have ceased to look.

The dulling of taste here referred to is of much relevance for artistic judgements. It was Karl Kraus who discovered and expounded the significance of banality, which is closely bound up with the innermost problems of contemporary moral and aesthetic life, with the dividing line between spiritual veracity and pretence. This is also the problem with which Adolf Loos grappled in his critique of our age, and from which he drew his conclusions for architecture.

5

'Children are the best educators, for they listen to one another more willingly and attentively and *speak* among themselves a more intelligible language than we do.' (Goethe, in conversation, 1824)

Unfruitful as Wittgenstein's teaching experience appears to have been for him, its influence on his development from the author of the *Tractatus* to that of the *Investigations* should not be underestimated, even though he would probably not have admitted it himself. When this man, who until then – for all the depth of his insight into the essence of life and humanity – had been frighteningly unworldly and hopelessly foreign to human society, was suddenly brought face to face with its grisly reality, he was luckily also brought into direct contact with children, which continued for several years. Although the schoolmaster, even at a primary school, hears only very occasionally how children talk among themselves – for the teacher is told nothing, unless they know the answer to one of his questions, and that answer again will not be given in the children's own language which they use among themselves.

Yet, for a number of years he was compelled to seek to translate the questions he had to ask as a teacher into a language which he could assume to come close to the children's language (their real one, not a pseudo-pedagogical one, which he would have abhorred). It seems to me that his much later attempt to convey in a new form the philosophical results of the *Tractatus*, corrected by fresh insights, bears witness to the influence of that period. And the outcome of that second venture might well have been different, and indeed less fruitful, if he had accepted the suggestion that he should return to Cambridge which was made to him immediately after the completion of the *Tractatus*. In Cambridge, too, he would have learnt from dialogue, but learnt less, for his students could only have made pathetic attempts to copy his own language, and he would never have been able in talking to them to cut loose from habitual forms.

Through that practical experience he had learnt that here also it would not be of decisive importance if his questions were merely asked and not answered, just as his questions to the children are likely to have been left mostly unanswered. In the *Tractatus* he had confined himself – rightly in view of its form – to giving answers to questions on what he had to communicate. But later he used the acquired art of asking questions with consummate skill, and the crucial simplicity with which he accomplished this in his profoundest mental probings constitutes his great new philosophical achievement, just as we may safely assume that, whatever the doubts and hindrances were at the time, it constituted his positive educational contribution to the children's exercises in thinking.

His later attempts to correct his earlier results, as formulated in the reflective monologues of the *Tractatus*, in the light of his later insights generally mark a transition from the categorical propositional form of statements to the Socratic form of questions.

I once heard a critic ask: When Wittgenstein ceased to examine the ideal language of philosophy and turned his attention to everyday speech, measuring the former by the yardstick of the latter, did he not overlook the fact that everyday speech itself is 'influenced' by more academic forms of language? Here we come up once more against the old fundamental misunderstanding. It was not Wittgenstein's intention at all to copy in his investigations of everyday speech the treatment he had so felicitously applied to the language of philosophy. Nobody felt as acutely as he that a dialogue with any language must be conducted on, and in, its own terms, as it were: if with the language of philosophy, then in the exactitude appropriate and essential to it; if with everyday language, then not, of course, in terms of deliberate imprecision (which would be fatuous) nor yet with exactitude (which would not work), but by abstaining altogether from answering it and merely asking questions in it. 'That done, things will sort themselves out.'[1]

Finally I wish to make some remarks about Russell's introduction to the *Tractatus* and Wittgenstein's relations with Moritz Schlick, the founder of the Vienna School.

6

My long silence mentioned in Wittgenstein's letter of 30th May 1920 (I. *32*) was probably due to the fact that I found it very hard to write to him in the particular circumstances, and – as so often happens in such cases – became paralysed by that feeling.

After my own unsuccessful attempts to get the book published, I was depressed when Wittgenstein – whatever his reason – was unwilling to seize an opportunity that

[1] A favourite quotation of Wittgenstein's, from *Eduards Traum* by Wilhelm Busch. In context it runs: 'And joking apart, my friends, only a man who has a heart can feel and say truly, indeed from the heart, that he is good for nothing. That done, things will sort themselves out.'

would never come again. Indeed, I still believe that the *Tractatus* would never have been published without Russell's introduction.

I was, of course, in no position to judge whether Wittgenstein's refusal was justified, as I did not know the text of the introduction to which he took exception. But had he shown it to me, had he even asked my advice, I should naturally, as always, have trusted his superior judgement. And retrospectively it is clear to me today that Wittgenstein had good reason for his negative reaction, which he himself, incidentally, did *not* carry to its practical conclusion as his first impulse had suggested.

Yet, Russell's introduction may be considered one of the main reasons why the book, though recognized to this day as an event of decisive importance in the field of logic, has failed to make itself understood as a philosophical work in the wider sense. Wittgenstein must have been deeply hurt to see that even such outstanding men, who were also helpful friends of his, were incapable of understanding his purpose in writing the *Tractatus*. And the deep depression manifest in his letters of the next few months – a depression that contributed to his decision to take up schoolmastering[1] – sprang from his doubt as to whether he would ever succeed in making himself understood as a philosopher.

7

The so-called 'Vienna Circle' was a philosophical circle of Vienna University, which had gathered round Professor Moritz Schlick. In 1926 Schlick met Wittgenstein, of

[1] Wittgenstein's decision to train as a teacher had of course been taken long before Russell's introduction reached him (cf. I. *21*). A letter to Russell of 19 August 1919 shows that Russell had already betrayed some misunderstanding. In the same letter Wittgenstein mentions that Frege had indicated that he did not understand a word of the book. (Part only of this letter has been published in *Notebooks 1914–1916*, pp. 129 f.) An earlier letter from the prison camp shows that Wittgenstein was quite sure his work would not be understood by anyone.

whom he had not heard before,[1] and his introduction to the ideas of the *Tractatus* through personal contact with the author did so much to clarify his own thought – which from the outset had not been opposed to Wittgenstein's – that these ideas now became, in Schlick's interpretation, the central theme of the group.

Schlick met Wittgenstein at the house of Wittgenstein's sister, Mrs. Stonborough, who had asked Schlick to tea (together with Professor Bühler, the psychologist, and Mrs. Bühler). Wittgenstein told me the next day: 'Each of us thought the other must be mad.' This ironical summing up suggests that Wittgenstein's laconic utterances, abrupt and paradoxical and ejaculated with great emphasis, must have struck Schlick at first as the behaviour of a presumptuous dilettante – a first impression very much like that of the musicians when Wittgenstein had butted in at their rehearsal. Afterwards Wittgenstein corrected his own first impression of Schlick and took the trouble to explain his ideas in detail, and Schlick, in turn, realized very quickly what sort of a man he had met.

Wittgenstein found Schlick a distinguished and understanding partner in discussion, all the more so because he appreciated Schlick's highly cultured personality – something which Wittgenstein always found essential in his intellectual contacts with others. Wittgenstein took no active part in the activities of Schlick's 'Circle', i.e. its seminars and discussions (and he is said to have been very rarely present at such events). It need not be added that the predominantly positivist tendency of that circle in matters outside pure logic did not appeal to him, and that, at the same time, he did not feel called upon to exert a corrective influence.

[1] Engelmann was misinformed on this point. For some further details of Wittgenstein's relation with Schlick, see the Editor's Appendix.

VI. *Wittgenstein's Family*

In the Anglo-Saxon world, where Wittgenstein's influence has so far been greatest, his personality cannot be understood without a closer acquaintance with the soil that nurtured his intellectual roots. Once seen in the environment of the Austrian-Jewish spirit, now long defunct, this enigmatic modern figure comes to life, and his features suddenly take on a familiar look.

Ludwig Wittgenstein (1889–1951) came from Vienna, and although he had his higher education in Britain and was in his later years professor of philosophy at Cambridge, he belongs unmistakably to the intellectual ambience of Vienna, not only as one of the last few men who truly understood the great figures of old Viennese culture (the great Brahms was a friend of his parents), but as the greatest offspring and antithesis of that closing epoch of Viennese-Jewish culture during the first quarter of our century when the light of European intellect shone with full brilliance for the last time, up to the present.

He came from a Jewish family but, like his father, Karl Wittgenstein, before him, was brought up in the Christian faith.[1] (The name is derived from a village in Hesse, itself named after the famous princely house of Wittgenstein, with which his family had no connection.) His mother was half-Jewish.

Karl Wittgenstein, who died in 1913, was an engineer by profession. He was the son of a wealthy family which, coming originally from Hesse, had lived in Austria since 1851. When he was a child, or possibly even before his birth, his father adopted the Christian faith. He himself became one of the founders of the Austrian iron industry and a millionaire.

[1] See Appendix for further remarks on Wittgenstein's family.

His essays in Vienna's leading daily, the *Neue Freie Presse*, show him as an economist of great breadth of vision and superior judgement. His was the superiority of the practitioner who has turned his insights into achievement over the luminaries of academic economics, whom he had every right to think little of (even though there existed at that period an eminent 'Vienna School' of economics which was decades ahead of its time).

I think I can recognize in Ludwig Wittgenstein's way of thinking, as applied to the problems of philosophy in the *Tractatus*, an unmistakable family likeness with his father's economic thinking. Karl Wittgenstein's articles, which attracted much notice and exercised considerable influence at the time, were later collected in a book printed in a private edition only. His fundamental insights, based on personal experience, would still be relevant today, for all the changes undergone by the world economy in over fifty years. A shrewd and judicious observer once said about him: Had Karl Wittgenstein lived in Germany rather than Austria, Bismarck would not have ignored such a man but appointed him to a position of authority in the state's economy.

If that did not happen in Austria, it was certainly not due to the family's predominantly Jewish origin, as an outsider might wrongly suppose. For not only the top ranks of the bourgeoisie but also large sections of the aristocratic families in Vienna and the whole of Austria had for generations absorbed so much Jewish blood that no invisible walls would have stood in his way. But when Karl Wittgenstein was offered the nobiliary 'von' – the goal which other Jewish millionaires of considerably lesser means desired, and usually attained – he turned it down, because he rightly felt that such behaviour, customary though it was at the time, was the mark of a parvenu. In his later years when, in keeping with his position, he still entertained on a lavish scale, at his truly princely house in the Alleegasse (built by a Count Nako), the family's isolation from this kind of life began to take shape, and after his death it became complete.

Wittgenstein's paternal grandmother came from the highly cultured Viennese family of Figdor. His maternal grandmother – and his only non-Jewish ancestor – came from a land-owning family in Southern Styria.

As a self-made man acutely conscious of the psychological difficulties liable to hamper the development of young people growing up in great wealth, Karl Wittgenstein brought up Ludwig and the other children in a way that to modern eyes may appear somewhat puritanical. Such treatment did not arouse resistance and resentment in Ludwig Wittgenstein with his tremendous inner resources – as it usually does with weaker natures – but it actually strengthened his loyalty towards all legitimate authority, whether religious or social. This attitude towards all *genuine* authority was so much second nature with him that revolutionary convictions of whatever kind appeared to him throughout his life simply as 'immoral'. This attitude, which would not have been particularly noteworthy in an ordinary person, turned that superior man, who saw through and abhorred all *unjustified* conventions, into a figure utterly beyond the comprehension of the 'educated' of our day – but also into an unattainable model and example for those capable of seeing below the surface.

One trait implanted in him by this disposition and education was his painstaking anxiety not to shirk, in deed or even in thought, any of the human or civic obligations which in our society can so often be bought off, wholly or in part, by the rich.

VII. *Kraus, Loos, and Wittgenstein*

It has been repeatedly emphasized here that Wittgenstein's true role and significance is different, indeed opposite, to what has been generally supposed. There are critics who reject his endeavours as a perilous tendency paving the way for a totally destructive intellectualism. Thanks to Wittgenstein, it is held, the 'irrational' voices of feeling and faith are to be silenced in philosophy, which is thus to share the fate of religion. This interpretation takes exception to present-day intellectualism – which I also consider the basic disease of our time – but defines this intellectualism as an excessive and one-sided preoccupation with intellectual activities. Now, this is both true and false. It is certainly not true that our age has too much intellect. After all, if a cook regularly puts too much salt in the soup, it is not because she keeps too large a salt jar in the cupboard but because she does not know how to handle salt. The intellectual (in the bad sense of the word) has not too much reason but too little judgement (mother wit, common sense). Grillparzer said about the Germans that they were possessed of reason wherever it was out of place.

In this sense it may be said that the attempt to engage in philosophy on a consciously one-sided logical basis is directed against feeling, intuition, the irrational, etc. *not* in general but only *where they are out of place*. And these vital values will not suffer through such a clean separation, indeed they will be quite as well, if not better, served by it than pure intellect and logic which, on the face of it, seem the only beneficiaries of this rescue operation. The mischief against which the *Tractatus* is directed is the mingling of the sciences with metaphysics. It is never against science 'in its right place'; for science, indeed, it reserves the entire field of 'language' as the realm of meaningful propositions. It is not against the universal (and legitimate) human urge to reach out for the metaphysical; but it is against the attempt to express it in meaningful propositions. For the metaphysical urge is 'out of place' when it poses an articulate question and attempts to give an answer, that is to say when it takes shape as philosophy.

Wittgenstein's attempt to draw a clear line between what can and what cannot be said is only one in a series of similar efforts. A comparison is instructive. Wittgenstein comes from Vienna, from an epoch which we must in retrospect regard as intellectually most productive. Comparison reveals an affinity of his ideas with those of two distinguished Viennese contemporaries, Karl Kraus and Adolf Loos. Indeed the basic tendencies of these three authors are the same.

2

When Wittgenstein went to Norway for the first time to find the tranquillity he needed for his concentrated mental labours, he was concerned about some remaining obscurities in the work of his first teachers, Russell and Frege, which he considered generally right and vastly superior to anything else he had read. He was convinced, no doubt, that it must be possible to put those points more clearly, and the major effort on which he set out was a passionate attempt to do just that.

He told me that he had Karl Kraus's *Die Fackel* sent to his address in Norway, which indicates that he had been a keen reader of that journal before leaving Vienna. I am convinced that the way of thinking which he found in Kraus's writings exercised a decisive and lasting influence on the objectives of his philosophical activity. Indeed, this influence goes much deeper than can ever be suspected by those who have not really understood what Kraus is really after (and that means the great majority, even of his regular readers and supporters). On the other hand Wittgenstein cared neither then nor later for most of the aspects of Kraus's achievement for which his readers admired him. (It is necessary for me here to discuss Kraus and what his ideas meant to Wittgenstein, so as to clarify this important point.)

Kraus is a polemical writer of matchless and devastating power, but owing to his peculiar cast of mind he can conceive and express an argument only with reference to particular individuals. This is as a rule a morally as well as intellectually dubious method, and one not without danger to the polemical author himself. With Kraus, however, the method is nearly always redeemed by a conscientiousness which treats any personal weakness of the adversary that is not given away in his language as taboo; and even more by the polemicist's confession that 'polemics are a mischief though the dictates of art may at times turn them into a necessity'.

The influence which Kraus exercised on Wittgenstein cannot easily be discerned at a first glance, because Wittgenstein does not display Kraus's most conspicuous trait of personal polemics. Wittgenstein's polemics are completely impersonal: the adversary he contends against in the *Tractatus* is philosophy itself. To avoid a gross misunderstanding of what is involved in Wittgenstein's debt to Kraus, the following points must be appreciated:

In his polemics Kraus resorts time and again to the technique of taking his victim 'at his word', that is, of driving home his accusation and exposing threadbare intentions by the simple means of citing the accused's own words and phrases. As Kraus in his *literary* polemic takes an individual adversary at his word, and through him indirectly a whole era, so Wittgenstein in his *philosophical* polemic takes 'language' itself (i.e. the language of philosophy) at its word. The crucial circumstance that, unlike Kant, he chooses to make not 'reason' but language the subject of his critique, is proof that he takes language at its word – or, more correctly, at its turn of phrase, its proposition: for the proposition is something tangible that, in contrast to reason, cannot escape our grip once we lay hands on it.

He investigates philosophically not this proposition or that but, logically, the proposition as such: he investigates what a proposition can, and what it cannot, say. And no matter whether or not he has succeeded in his intended frontier demarcation, by the mere act of asking the question he gets to the bottom of a philosophical confusion that had persisted for centuries. (And he arrives at a negative answer – though the *Tractatus* does not say so explicitly – to the question which the *Critique of Pure Reason* had set out to answer in the affirmative: Do 'synthetic a priori propositions' exist?)

I guess that the statement of the *Tractatus*, 'Ethics and aesthetics are one',[1] is one of the most frequently misunderstood propositions of the book. Surely it cannot be assumed that this wide-ranging and profound thinker had meant to say that there is no difference at all between ethics and aesthetics! But the statement is put in parentheses, said by the way, as something not really meant to be uttered, yet something that should not be passed over in silence at that point. And this is done in the form of a reminder recalling to the understanding reader an insight which he is *assumed* to possess in any case. Seen from a different angle, the insight into the fundamental connection between aesthetics (logic as well, it would appear) and ethics is also a basic element in Kraus's critique of poetic language.

Kraus was (after Weininger) the first to raise an earnest voice of warning, reminding an epoch given to judging life as well as art by one-sided aesthetic canons that the

[1] Pears & McGuinness: 'one and the same'.

morality of an artist is vital to his work. Kraus did this most clearly in his essay 'Heine and the Consequences'.

The point, however, that is so often misunderstood and where misunderstanding has given rise to hopelessly confused aesthetic misjudgements is this: in the contemplation of art the moral approach is in order only when a moral defect is *manifest* in the artist's work. And here it is Kraus's decisive achievement to have demonstrated that, as far as language is concerned, this is nearly always the case. 'I cannot get myself to accept that a whole sentence can ever come from half a man.' This shows that Kraus adopts the only attitude that makes sense by judging the morality not of an individual act, but of the person acting, and it is the latter which is unerringly revealed to Kraus through language.

Kraus sees the difference between Heine and his greater contemporary and fellow-Parisian Baudelaire revealed in the comparison between Heine's moral levity and Baudelaire's passionate avowal of his own sinfulness, which he experienced and proclaimed with equal passion and self-destructive ardour. Now Heine's moral levity matters because it is identical with the levity of his approach to language, above all his lyrical language. That is where Kraus exposed it, so that it has by now become visible to many. Just as Matthias Claudius reveals his deep and simple faith in the poem 'The moon has risen in the sky' ('Der Mond ist aufgegangen').

In a situation in which the journalistic practice of mixing news with comment and the falsification of genuine ideas by clichés threatens public life with spiritual and eventually physical corruption, Karl Kraus strives to preserve the purity of a language born of creative poetical experience, and akin in its vital force to the simple forms of speech used by unspoilt people. But the poet's language is precisely the form of statement which Wittgenstein seeks to banish from philosophy.

In his critique of language Kraus shows indefatigable solicitude 'for the comma'. This should not be seen as a solicitude extending to the most unimportant, but as a solicitude for the most important though least conspicuous. The comma is essential, for here the sentence, the logical element of language, is at stake. And he discovered that something is fundamentally amiss with the sentences, the periods, printed today in literary works and the press as well as with those used in everyday speech; that violations of the grammar of language point to similar violations of the grammar of logic; and that defects of thought show up moral defects. The picture of the general spiritual condition of modern man thus revealed led Kraus to speak of 'the death of the world in the death of the mind'. To him also the only decisive point is not what the language of modern man *says*, but what it makes *manifest* without his intention.

3

Adolf Loos in his turn (he once said to Wittgenstein: 'You are me!') counters the ever-renewed attempts of the architects of his time either to revive old forms or invent new and supposedly modern ones with *his* demand: to be silent where one cannot speak; to do no more than design a building with technical correctness, guided by the right human approach, and leave the right and truly modern form to emerge *spontaneously*. This form should not be proclaimed explicitly and purposefully in the architect's design of an article of daily use or a building, but should be *manifest* in it.

'The path is this: God created the artist, the artist creates his age, the age creates the artisan, the artisan creates the button.' This is Loos's basic insight into the connection between the crafts and art. It is directed above all against the notion of 'arts-and-crafts', predominant in Central Europe from about 1895 to 1930, which Loos made it his life's task to combat in the fields of domestic architecture and industrial design. It was the aim of arts-and-crafts to overcome the rationalized, one-sidedly technological form of industrial production and put in its place a more ideal, but in principle impossible, 'revival' of a mode of production meant to sublimate and spiritualize the technical necessities of design by refurbishing outworn patterns or re-inventing forgotten ones.

Here Loos states an insight that is closely akin to the tendency of the *Tractatus*. Translated into its terms, Loos's insight can be put as follows: The 'arts-and-crafts' tendency that has sought, ever since the Renaissance, to imbue the scientific (technical-artisan) view of the world with a higher spiritual dignity, is here represented by philosophy, and the 'philosopher' seeks again and again to achieve new and higher forms by smuggling in explicit statements of the unutterable (the very target of Wittgenstein's attack, first in the *Tractatus* and later in his academic teaching).

'New forms? How dull! It is the new spirit that matters. Even out of old forms it will fashion what we new men need' (Adolf Loos). It is *not new shapes of things, not new philosophical systems* that are needed to express a truly new spirit capable of leading to new ways of *life*.

Loos was imbued with the conviction that the true artist was far ahead of his time and could not be understood at first by his contemporaries. Yet he would surely have resisted strenuously the conclusion that this insight should serve as a licence for arrogant nonentities and a pretext giving the incompetent a semblance of justification for riding at least temporarily on the wave of what is still uncomprehended. Proceeding from his basic view (quoted above) that there is no direct path from art to craft, since between them stands the age as it is today, Loos carried out his main purpose of a clean intellectual separation between art and craft. But his insight into the nature of the crafts, in which he includes domestic architecture, also shows a way to combat all false tendencies within art, which seek time after time to establish a so-called 'modern' art which must at any price differ from the old. 'I have more affinity with truth, though it be centuries old, than with the lie strutting by my side' (Adolf Loos).

According to the shallow and half-baked ideas of would-be creators of new art who had not grasped the separation between art and crafts, it was supposed to be possible to blaze an aesthetic trail, beginning with art and leading eventually to new ways of life for the individual and society. Since Ruskin and Emerson, generations of artists have sought to breathe a new spirit into the withered life of industrial society by means of loftier aesthetic forms. The methods used in the attempt to achieve this end have varied from decade to decade, but the effect has every time been disastrously negative: the growth of queer hermit centres away from the main stream of events, exhausting themselves in pre-dictably impotent attempts to make permanent changes, however slight, in the existing state of affairs.

It is as mistaken to look upon Loos as a representative of the *Neue Sachlichkeit* movement as to take Wittgenstein for a positivist. Loos shares with *Neue Sachlichkeit* the hatred of the superfluous, which can stifle the essential with its rank growth. But this hatred springs from very different roots in the case of *Neue Sachlichkeit*, as propagated and practised by Loos's chief antagonists and chief imitators, the architects of the Dessau Bauhaus. To them it is first of all an aesthetic affair, and they turn simplicity into a fetish; they adorn themselves with the plain and unadorned, and thereby only render it inessential and more super-fluous than the superfluities they had set out to remove.

'All that Adolf Loos and I — he materially and I verbally — have ever meant to say is that there is a difference between an urn and a chamber-pot. But the people of today can be divided into those who use the chamber-pot as an urn and those who use the urn as a chamber-pot' (Karl Kraus).

This distinction also figures in Kraus's view – which may have seemed paradoxical at the time – on the relative merits of Vienna and Berlin. It goes without saying that for Kraus, as for anyone who is not culturally blind, the values formerly represented by Vienna (from Haydn to Schubert and Raimund) reach standards out of comparison with anything ever offered by Berlin. But Kraus's indignation was aroused when he saw that those values, which by his time had mostly been dead for half a century, preserved only in the noble mummy of a partly intact townscape, were now being claimed by the living Vienna as the hallmark of its own worth, and continually invoked by those least qualified against any judgement in favour of Berlin. A city like Berlin, which neither has nor, on the whole, claims cultural brilliance is for all its baseness still preferable in Kraus's eyes to the arrogated bogus culture – a culture turned into its opposite, misused as ornament and mask – that is the culture of contemporary Vienna. All things considered, life is more nearly bearable in the other environment.

Here we have a complete paradigm of the tendency of the *Tractatus*: the higher sphere, which demands defence in an age that denies it, is made yet more suspect by threadbare verities and proofs unfitted for such a rescue operation.

Thus it is the motive of Kraus and Loos also to uphold the distinction – now lost and beyond the comprehension of our age – between the higher and lower spheres. All human culture is based on faith in the existence of a higher sphere. The Enlightenment, beginning in the eighteenth century, sought to 'prove' that the higher sphere did not exist but was a mere illusion, which it set out to destroy. Its method was to apply the principle of development with the greatest possible consistency, contending that all entities we assign to the higher sphere have 'developed' from things in the lower sphere. In this way, the Enlightenment believes, the sublime has been 'unmasked' as a product of development, and thereby as base.

The method used by Kraus and Loos is to present afresh the sublime that exists in art: this is their proof of the existence of the higher sphere ('The artist must create, not speak' – Goethe). Kraus attempts to do this by creative literary works (which, of course, he did not write to prove his point, but which, having created them, he produced in evidence).

What Kraus, Loos, and Wittgenstein have in common is their endeavour to separate and divide correctly. They are creative separators. It is understandable that they should arouse fierce resistance, since their endeavour runs counter to the deepest (and justified) instinct of their age, which seeks to overcome division in all fields. Yet division can be overcome only through a new unity built on fresh foundations, never through an indiscriminate mixture of polluted and deformed debris, the detritus of once living cultural values. There are truly serious metaphysicians who seek to overcome division precisely by striving after such a new standpoint. It can be tried. But it seems to me that such a new beginning lies in the future and cannot, on the whole, be the task of our time. It is true, the task seems pressing. Yet it may be better to hold back for a while, for the attempts to achieve a separation and thus to obtain some constituent parts in a pure form, must come first and cannot be skipped.

It must be emphasized that in dealing with the first task, 'not to deny the seeds of a new culture, but search for them or help to create them', we must not neglect the second task, of combating 'inferior tendencies posing as the true heirs'. It is against such tendencies that the work of the separators is directed.

That seers have seen and thinkers have thought does not, in itself, achieve anything. It needs the work of a generation to bring these thoughts to fruition in all spheres of life. Men like Wittgenstein, Kraus, and Loos have created the possibility. To convert possibilities into fact is the programme of positive intellectual work. It is not right to argue: 'This has been said before; let us pass on to the next business! Is there anything new?' The right attitude answers: It has only been said. Now comes the work of understanding it in all its consequences and applying it.

The common core of these three thinkers is their insistence on truth and clarity, and this seems to me precisely what is missing in the cultural efforts of our age, and which, therefore, it should be the first and foremost task of all men dedicated to culture to emphasize in all spheres of intellectual and artistic activity.

VIII. *Wordless Faith*

The 'recasting of all values' in which Nietzsche saw the only hope for a survival of human culture cannot in reality mean anything except the decontamination of intellectual life by purging it of empty phrases.

The ideal strivings of human society, culminating in socialism on the one hand and nationalism on the other, must in future be acted out, not talked about.

It is not true that their realization requires a preliminary stage of talking and writing in the present-day sense, let alone in the present-day volume. The essential core which must be communicated is but a negligible fraction of the words churned out to this end today. The necessary talking, which can be and should be a realization of the spirit and not a cheap substitute, is drowned today in a spate of verbiage and clichés.

In the first place, 'ideals' themselves, insofar as they are meant seriously as something to be translated into reality, cannot be communicated by words. They are of the spirit, and can be indestructibly demonstrated only by making them real. What still needs to be said after that by way of showing, explaining, teaching can be done in relatively few words. Only in this way can 'the word' be restored to the value, the weight, that belongs to it by right.

Theodor Häcker, the translator of Kierkegaard, rightly attaches much of the blame for the continuing spiritual impoverishment of society to the film (he was referring to the silent film, but in the sound film the word is no more than a barely noticed background noise), and he is equally right in interpreting the way in which the general interest has here shifted from the printed word to the picture as one of the main symptoms of spiritual destruction. Yet this general estrangement from the word is an estrangement from the *devalued*, not the living word!

Propaganda, the main instrument for the dissemination of social ideals, consists almost entirely of clichés. This cannot be countered, however, by an 'abolition' of propaganda, but only by a cliché-free propaganda that will never speak about ideals unless it is necessary, and will then speak little. Propaganda today is synonymous with falsehood and catch phrases. But why should it not be possible, in principle, once the cliché has been killed, to present propaganda for the good? And if humanity has learned today to lie by machine, why should it not be possible in future to spread the truth by machine? Not until the word is prized again as the treasure it is, instead of being treated as a shoeshine rag, can it regain its power to move the world.

Everyone who writes must be educated to test each word for its true weight before writing it down and always to select the expression that has no more weight than is appropriate for that which is to be said. And the reader must be trained to weigh words correctly, even, indeed primarily, where the writer does not drive his point home with a sledge-hammer.

The intellectual step forward that is needed is the recognition that if new ways of life are to arise in our epoch of hopelessly tangled and confused ideologies, it is not merely *one* possibility but the *only* conceivable possibility that they should arise without waiting for a new ideology to be stated and communicated first. If tenable, the new ways will, on the contrary, reveal and manifest the new ideology which – unspoken – had formed their basis all the time and without which they could not have materialized.

Indeed, the transference of all metaphysical essences to the realm of the unutterable has for the first time created the possibility of a universal human way of life without a *denial of metaphysical beliefs*.

Today the eastern world is still locked in battle with the

West for the realization of their ideologies. Yet it would be possible for the two ideologies to find a common basis and go a long distance together before their ways must part. And perhaps, when the crossroads was reached, they need not part at all.

So the spiritual task of our time is to find the neutral way of life which can be accepted by either side without denying its ideology, and which will make it *possible to erect what is of necessity a provisional emergency building* as a temporary home for human society until a genuine edifice can be built to last for generations to come.

Wittgenstein himself would undoubtedly have rejected such an account of his aims as a psychologizing falsification of his ideas. He would have insisted that what he had to say was just what his propositions expressed and *no more;* and if the propositions failed to express it, then the expression was simply wrong and the propositions concerned were worthless.

What Wittgenstein's life and work shows is the possibility of a new *spiritual attitude*. It is 'a new way of life' which he lived, and because of which he has so far not been understood. For a new way of life entails a new language. His way of life is the same as that of some great men of the past, but its special significance for us lies in the fact that only in our epoch has this example come to point the way to a universal new way of life.

Wittgenstein's language is the language of wordless faith. Such an attitude adopted by other individuals of the right stature will be the source from which new forms of society will spring, forms that will need no verbal communication, because they will be lived and thus made manifest. In the future, ideals will not be communicated by attempts to describe them, which inevitably distort, but by the models of an appropriate conduct in life.

And such exemplary lives will be of incomparable value educationally; no doctrine conveyed in words can be a substitute for them. For even if such communication should succeed to the extent of enabling those who have already grasped its point through personal experience to apply it and realize it in their own lives, the fact remains – of which historical instances abound – that any doctrine uttered in words is the source of its own misconstruction by worshippers, disciples, and supporters. It is they who have so far without exception robbed all doctrines laid down in words of their effect, and who always threaten to turn the blessing into a curse. Other dangers may be inherent in wordless faith (dangers from which no human enterprise is exempt, and which may become apparent only in the future); but from *that* fundamental danger it will be free.

Editor's Appendix

The best supplement to Engelmann's memoir, indeed the background against which he intended it to be seen, is the *Biographical Sketch* (Oxford, 1958) by Professor von Wright. This appendix deals with a few biographical questions raised by the memoir and not already settled there.[1]

Wittgenstein's family (Chapter VI)

Both of Wittgenstein's paternal grandparents, Hermann Christian (1803–78) and his wife Fanny, were Protestants, the former baptized in childhood, the latter before marriage. Hermann Christian, though born in Hesse was, at the time of his marriage (1839), a woolmerchant in Leipzig. Eight or nine of his eleven children, including Karl (1847–1913), were born there before he moved to Austria (1851), where he bought, leased, and managed landed property and was very successful. His eight daughters and three sons, carefully educated and simply brought up, became remarkable for their gifts of character, for their part in the cultural life of Vienna, and for their charitable works. Wittgenstein was brought up in this extended family, which was multiply intermarried with the Franz's, leaders of the Protestant community. Among his uncles by marriage he numbered a Catholic general and distinguished officials, judges, and scientists of Austrian or German descent. His own official religion was

[1] I am much indebted to a number of friends and relations of Wittgenstein's for information, notably to Professor H. Hänsel, Mr. L. Ficker, Mr. R. Koder, Mr. A. Sjögren, Dr. T. Stonborough and Mr. J. Stonborough. Professor F. A. von Hayek very generously put at my disposal material he had collected himself. The families of the late Mrs. Margaret Stonborough and the late Mrs. Blanche Schlick have kindly allowed me to quote from letters. For statements of fact and expressions of opinion alike the entire responsibility is of course mine.
. [Ludwig Ficker died at the age of 86 while this book was in the press.]

Roman Catholicism, which he owed to his mother, the Jewish side of her family having been Christian for some generations.

The cultural life of Vienna owed much to persons of Jewish descent. In some cases, such as those of Otto Weininger and Karl Kraus, both of whom Wittgenstein admired, it is possible to discern the influence of a specifically Jewish environment and certainly they were conscious of it. But Wittgenstein's own ancestry seems to have been too remote to affect him in this way and was more or less forgotten until the *Anschluß*.

Engelmann's description of Karl Wittgenstein as a self-made man may seem surprising in view of the family's prosperity. I believe that it is not a slip but a reference to his exceptional independence of spirit. This led him to run away to America as a boy (he had not been successful at the classical *Gymnasium*) and support himself for a year, even saving some money, as a waiter, bar-tender, violinist and teacher of German and of mathematics. After his return he studied engineering for a while but hardly practised it, being soon engaged in the management of a steel firm whose managing director was related to him by marriage and gaining a great fortune by bold but justified reliance on his own judgement. It is possible to see the influence of his own youth in the education he chose for his older children, employing tutors rather than sending them to school and preferring technical training to the development of their artistic gifts. It seems that tragic experience led to a change in this policy. At any rate Ludwig, the youngest child, was sent to the Linz *Realschule*[1] at the age of 14 and Paul, the second youngest, became a concert pianist.

Paul (1887–1961) will perhaps serve as an example of the remarkable assembly of gifts which marked Wittgenstein's own generation. He was a talented pianist who lost

[1] i.e. a school where Latin and Greek were not taught. Wittgenstein's marks there were not particularly good, except in religious knowledge.

an arm in the First World War, but by dint of that determination and self-mastery which had supported his father in America he taught himself to play with one arm and resumed his career with great success.

Wittgenstein's meetings with Ficker and Loos (Chapters II. 3, IV. 2, and VII)

The exact date of Wittgenstein's meeting with Loos and the background of some remarks in I. 5 are given in an article by Mr. Ludwig Ficker[1] in the last number of *Der Brenner*.[2] Wittgenstein had been impressed by Karl Kraus's praise of *Der Brenner* (which Kraus called 'the only honest periodical in Austria, and hence the only honest periodical in Germany') and turned to Ficker for help in distributing anonymously 100,000 kr. (then the equivalent of £4,167) from the money he had inherited from his father. Rilke and Trakl were the first beneficiaries that occurred to Ficker and each received a fifth of the whole sum. Except for insisting on a contribution to *Der Brenner* itself, Wittgenstein would take no part in selecting the beneficiaries: hence his remark about Ehrenstein in I. 5. Wittgenstein admired Trakl's poems and spoke most warmly of some that Rilke sent him through Ficker, but was not very impressed by the expressions of gratitude that reached him from some of the others.

Wittgenstein first met Ficker on 26 July 1914 and Ficker introduced him to Loos on the next day. The two immediately engaged in a conversation on architectural questions as animated as Loos's deafness would allow. The house that Wittgenstein built in 1926–28 has some features reminiscent of Loos's work—the lack of ornament and the use of interlocking split-levels to prevent the division of the interior

[1] After the First World War the nobiliary particle was legally abolished in Austria.

[2] 'Rilke und der unbekannte Freund', *Der Brenner*, 18 (1954) pp. 234–48. I have also to thank Mr. Ficker and Mr. Walter Methlagl of Innsbruck for oral information and for showing me letters.

space into 'floors'—but in other respects—notably the tall and narrow windows and doors—it is very unlike that work. It is sad not to have Engelmann's account of the building of this house.

From the army Wittgenstein wrote often to Ficker until the latter was called up in late 1915. His letters, both then and after the war, have that directness and openness which made Wittgenstein's friendship so prized a possession. They show (as does his expression of concern in I. *28*) that his relations with Ficker must not be judged by his remarks in I. *41* and *45* alone.

Wittgenstein's military career
It may be useful to give the bare facts of Wittgenstein's war service here, partly since they serve to date his acquaintance with Engelmann. He enlisted in a garrison artillery regiment (*FsAR* 2) on 7 August 1914. He reached the front on 19 August and was employed in a humble capacity on a vessel in the Vistula until 10 December, thus taking part in the fluctuating fighting of that autumn in Galicia. He was then employed in an artillery workshop in Cracow, where his engineering skill was noticed and the Commandant gave him, quite irregularly, the status of an officer. After the break-through at Gorlice-Tarnow he was occasionally moved forward and from about the end of July 1915 was stationed at Sokal, north of Lwow, with the Artillery Workshop train. In early 1916 the efforts of the workshop Commandant to have Wittgenstein's position regularized failed and he had to be posted elsewhere. He went, as he had long wished, to the front, being attached on 21 March 1916 to a howitzer regiment (*FHR* 5, later *FAR* 105) based on Sanok, also in Galicia. He was employed as an artillery observer and soon won promotion to non-commissioned rank (*Vormeister*, 1 June). In the first days of the Brusilov offensive (4 June 1916) he won a decoration for bravery, evidently not for the first time, apparently in the particularly

heavy fighting south of Okna. He was promoted *Corporal* on 1 September, and won further decorations on 6 and 19 October. It must have been shortly after this that he went to Olmütz for training as an artillery officer (not in 1915, *pace* von Wright, op. cit., p. 8). He received the acting rank of *Fähnrich i.d.R.* on 1 December 1916 and that of *Leutnant i.d.R.* on 1 February 1918. He had returned to his regiment by 26 January 1917, and seems to have been involved mostly in static warfare in Bukovina until the Kerensky offensive of July 1917 when his regiment fell back to the line of the river Łomnica and then counter-attacked, taking part in the final recapture of Czernowitz. From then until the effective cessation of hostilities in that area he was involved in static warfare round Czernowitz, though taking part in an attack on Bojan to the east on 27 August (the date of I. 7). Olmütz was more conveniently situated than Vienna for leave and Wittgenstein must have been there at least once on leave, probably before July.

In spring 1918 Wittgenstein was moved to the south front and temporarily attached to a mountain artillery regiment (*GAR* 11). He was employed in the Asiago area and one of his many decorations was won on the first day of the last Austrian offensive in that region (15 June 1918). In July and perhaps August Wittgenstein was on leave in the Salzburg area and in Vienna. It seems to have been in this period that the final typescript of the *Tractatus* was made. Wittgenstein then returned to the front and he was made a prisoner of war, along with the bulk of the Austrian troops in that area, at Trent on 3 November 1918.

It will be seen that Wittgenstein had a most exacting war. The especial difficulties of inadequate supply and organization under which the Austro-Hungarian troops suffered, the misery of the civil population and of Russian prisoners in Galicia, and the hardships of the mountain fighting in the Asiago district are recognized by military historians. These were the background to the composition of the *Tractatus*.

The various military citations and reports concerning Wittgenstein and some reminiscences by fellow-soldiers show, as might be expected, that he stood out as a man of education and culture. Yet he is described as '*guter Kamerad*'. There is no trace of that difficulty in relations with his fellow men that troubled him later in the villages. In this respect the harsh circumstances of the war seem to have imposed a naturalness and a freedom from artificiality which were congenial to him. On troops under his command he had a good effect, particularly in battle, calming them and getting the best out of them, principally by reason of his own ability to continue steadily with his tasks as artillery observer even under heavy fire. It is natural to suppose that the hardships and effort of those years were partly responsible for the withdrawal from the world and the search for peace of the years that followed, though Wittgenstein himself would have been more likely to ascribe them to inner reasons.

The publication of the Tractatus

The offer of the *Tractatus* to Ficker was Wittgenstein's fourth attempt to have it published. He had sent it to Jahoda immediately it was finished (I. *16*) and to Braumüller immediately on his return from captivity (I. *21*). He told Ficker that Braumüller, to whom Russell had sent a letter recommending the book, would have published it, if Wittgenstein would pay for the paper and the printing, an arrangement which he rejected on principle. Frege had had a copy at least as early as Russell and though he gave Wittgenstein the impression that he had not understood a word of it, he seems to have promoted its publication. At any rate Wittgenstein told Ficker of a German professor who had given it to a friend, the editor of 'a sort of philosophical periodical' (perhaps *Beiträge zur Philosophie des deutschen Idealismus*, where Frege's post-war papers were published). This editor wanted changes in the book which

Wittgenstein refused to consider. Ficker could not himself grasp the significance of Wittgenstein's work and the precarious finances of *Der Brenner* forbade him to take the risk of publishing it himself. He enlisted the help of Rilke, who offered to approach Insel-Verlag and Otto Reichel of Darmstadt (Keyserling's publisher). When Russell offered to write an introduction, the publication of the book seemed assured and Ficker abandoned these efforts.

In the event Reclam would evidently not publish it without Russell's introduction, and Wittgenstein seems to have done nothing further. The publication by Ostwald over a year later was arranged by Russell (Wittgenstein did not read the proofs), as was the English publication, for which Wittgenstein corrected the version printed by Ostwald and the proofs of the translation by C. K. Ogden and F. P. Ramsey. Ramsey, when he got in touch with Wittgenstein in 1923, was congratulated on an excellent translation.

Most interesting is the description of the *Tractatus* that Wittgenstein gave to Ficker, which agrees with the impression of the work that Engelmann received. Wittgenstein described it as a strictly philosophical work which was at the same time literary. Ficker would not understand it though its content was in fact not remote from his own concerns.

The book's point is an ethical one. I once meant to include in the preface a sentence which is not in fact there now but which I will write out for you here, because it will perhaps be a key to the work for you. What I meant to write, then, was this: My work consists of two parts: the one presented here plus all that I have *not* written. And it is precisely this second part that is the important one.[1] My book draws limits to the sphere of the ethical from the inside as it were, and I am convinced that this is the ONLY *rigorous* way of drawing those limits. In short, I believe that where *many* others today are just *gassing*, I have managed in my book to put everything firmly into place by being silent about it.

[1] It is not clear where the self-quotation ends.

And for that reason, unless I am very much mistaken, the book will say a great deal that you yourself want to say. Only perhaps you won't see that it is said in the book. For now, I would recommend you to read the *preface* and the *conclusion*, because they contain the most direct expression of the point of the book.[1]

Wittgenstein's movements from 1919–26

The external facts of Wittgenstein's life during these years can best be given schematically:

1919–20 (academic year)	Teachers' Training College, Kundmanngasse, Vienna III.
December 1919	Visit to the Hague and meeting with Russell.
Summer 1920	Gardener at Klosterneuburg, near Vienna.
1920–21 & 1921–22 (academic years)	Elementary school teacher at Trattenbach, N.Ö.
Summer 1921	Visit to Norway with A. Sjögren.

[1] The remark about the literary character of the work comes from one undated letter. The other remarks, and the above quotation, from a slightly later undated one. Probably both date from September–October 1919. The German original of the quotation runs as follows (I am, as throughout, indebted to Wittgenstein's executors, for permission to quote the letter; Dr. Furtmüller has helped me with the translation):

. . . der Sinn des Buches ist ein ethischer. Ich wollte einmal in das Vorwort einen Satz geben, der nun tatsächlich nicht darin steht, den ich Ihnen aber jetzt schreibe weil er Ihnen vielleicht ein Schlüssel sein wird: Ich wollte nämlich schreiben, mein Werk bestehe aus zwei Teilen: aus dem, der hier vorliegt, und aus alledem, was ich *nicht* geschrieben habe. Und gerade dieser zweite Teil ist der Wichtige. Es wird nämlich das Ethische durch mein Buch gleichsam von Innen her begrenzt; und ich bin überzeugt, daß es, *streng*, NUR so zu begrenzen ist. Kurz, ich glaube: Alles das, was *viele* heute *schwefeln*, habe ich in meinem Buch festgelegt, indem ich darüber schweige. Und darum wird das Buch, wenn ich mich nicht sehr irre, vieles sagen, was Sie selbst sagen wollen, aber Sie werden vielleicht nicht sehen, daß es darin gesagt ist. Ich würde Ihnen nun empfehlen das *Vorwort* und den *Schluß* zu lesen, da diese den Sinn am Unmittelbarsten zum Ausdruck bringen.

Summer 1922	Meeting with Russell at Innsbruck.
Autumn 1922	Attached briefly to a secondary school at Hassbach, near Neunkirchen, N.Ö.
1922–23 & 1923–24 (academic years)	Elementary school teacher at Puchberg-am-Schneeberg, N.Ö.
September 1923	Visit of Ramsey to Puchberg.
March–October 1924	Ramsey in Vienna: a number of visits to Puchberg.
1924–25 (academic year) 1925–April 1926	Elementary school teacher at Otterthal, N.Ö.
Summer 1925	Visit to England (principally Manchester and Cambridge).
Spring–summer 1926	Gardener at Hütteldorf, near Vienna.
Autumn 1926	Work on the house in the Kundmanngasse starts.

His thoughts and activities during this time are briefly described in vonWright's *Biographical Sketch* and by G. Pitcher, *The Philosophy of Wittgenstein* (1964). In the fuller treatment which he planned to give of Wittgenstein's life as a schoolmaster Engelmann would doubtless have been able to show more adequately how Wittgenstein's numerous interests lightened to some extent the gloom which had settled over him and which is so apparent in his letters to Engelmann. He was very absorbed in the practical tasks of teaching and would take immense pains in preparing his work and in looking after the interests of his pupils. It is true that he did not find it easy to live among the farmers of these villages, but even there he made friends among his colleagues and neighbours, and friends also visited him. With these, with his favourite authors, and in music he found some peace. To those who knew him then it did not seem a time of unrelieved unhappiness, and some of those who derived most from knowing him came to know him precisely during that period.

Wittgenstein's meeting with Schlick (Chapter V. 7)
Engelmann was quite certainly mistaken in supposing that Schlick had never heard of Wittgenstein when he first met him. By 1926–27 the *Tractatus* was an object of lively interest in Vienna. The mathematician Hans Hahn had given a seminar on it in 1922 and both Schlick and Professor Kurt Reidemeister, the mathematician, who were called to Vienna in 1922, had been deeply impressed by it. Schlick wrote to Wittgenstein on 25 December 1924:

As an admirer of your *Tractatus Logico-Philosophicus* I have long intended to get in touch with you. My professorial and other duties are responsible for the fact that I have again and again put off carrying out my intention, though nearly five semesters have passed since I was called to Vienna. Every winter semester I have regular meetings with colleagues and gifted students who are interested in the foundations of logic and mathematics and your name has often been mentioned in this group, particularly since my mathematical colleague Professor Reidemeister reported on your work in a lecture which made a great impression on us all. So there are a number of people here—I am one of them myself— who are convinced of the importance and correctness of your fundamental ideas and who feel a strong desire to play some part in making your views more widely known . . . ⟨Schlick proceeds to ask how to obtain copies of the *Tractatus*⟩ . . . It would be an especially great pleasure for me actually to meet you and I should like to call on you sometime in Puchberg,[1] unless you let me know that you would rather not have your country retreat disturbed.

Wittgenstein found this letter in Otterthal on his return from the Christmas holidays and replied (7 January 1925) in most friendly terms, explaining that he himself had no copy of the *Tractatus*. He expressed great pleasure at the prospect of a visit from Schlick, who in his reply (14

[1] Wittgenstein had actually moved to Otterthal in the autumn.

146

January) once more expressed his intention of coming. In fact, it seems that he did not attempt the visit until after April 1926, for, when he and a few chosen pupils went to Otterthal, they found that Wittgenstein had given up his post as a teacher and left. For all Wittgenstein's good will towards Schlick, he was evidently too retiring to call on him, though Schlick had told him that he would of course be delighted to see him if he ever came to Vienna.

From the autumn of 1926 Wittgenstein was in Vienna engaged on the building of the house in the Kundmanngasse for his sister, Mrs. Margaret Stonborough. Mrs. Stonborough was well known in social and intellectual circles in Vienna and, in the event, it was through her that Schlick came to meet Wittgenstein. He had sent Wittgenstein one of his writings and he proposed a meeting with one or two other persons to discuss logical problems. Mrs. Stonborough wrote (19 February 1927):

He asks me to give you his warmest regards and to make his excuses to you, since he still feels quite unable to concentrate on logical problems as well as doing his present work, which demands all his energies. He could certainly not have a meeting with a number of people. He feels that if it were with you alone, dear Professor Schlick, he might be able to discuss such matters. It would then become apparent, he thinks, whether he is at present at all capable of being of use to you in this connexion.

Accordingly Schlick was invited to lunch, in order to discuss the matter afterwards.

Mrs. Stonborough's invitation ⟨Mrs. Schlick recalled⟩ brought with it a great joy and anticipation and this time M.'s expectations and hopes were not thwarted. Again ⟨as on the occasion of the abortive visit to Otterthal⟩ I observed with interest the reverential attitude of the pilgrim. He returned in an ecstatic state, saying little, and I felt I should not ask questions.[1]

[1] My account of Schlick's attempts to meet Wittgenstein and his eventual success is based, after the contemporary letters quoted above, on the recollections of the late Mrs. Blanche Schlick as given to Professor F. A. von Hayek and (in much smaller measure) to myself, through the good offices of Professor Kraft.

The slight variations in the different accounts of the circumstances of this meeting are hardly of importance. Wittgenstein's reactions are no doubt described correctly by Engelmann. Later conversations with Schlick and his circle are described, and in some cases transcribed in *Wittgenstein und der Wiener Kreis* (Oxford, forthcoming).

Index

Anscombe, Miss G. E. M., xi, xiv

Beethoven, 89
Bible, The, 8 f., 111 f.
Brahms, 6 f.
Braumüller, Wilhelm, 18 f., 142
Brenner, Der, 28 f., 43–5, 139, 143
Busch, Wilhelm, 116

Claudius, Matthias, 126

Dostoevsky, 26 f., 80

Ehrenstein, Albert, 4 f., 85, 139
Eng, Peter, 65 f.

Fackel, Die, 4 f., 123
Ficker, Ludwig (von), 26–9, 42 f., 48 f., 63, 139 f., 142–4
Frege, Gottlob, 16 f., 38 f., 95 f., 142

Goethe, 5 f., 87, 95, 114
Grillparzer, 87 f., 92, 122
Groag, Heinrich, 4–7, 24 f., 65

Häcker, Theodor, 133
Heine, 126
Hertz, Heinrich, 96
Hölderlin, 88, 93

Ibsen, 46 f.

Jahoda, Georg, 14 f.

Kant, 99, 108
Keller, Gottfried, 61, 86 f.
Keynes, J. M., 54 f.
Keyserling, Count Hermann, 36 f., 143
King of the Dark Chamber, The, 46 f.
Kraus, Karl, ix f., 14 f., 71, 82, 84, 86, 114, 123–7, 130, 138

149